Exploring
God's Creation
The Christian Liberty Press
Science Program

consultants and reviewers:

Dr. Paul Lindstrom
Michael McHugh

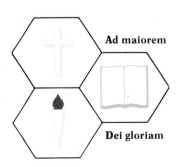

Ad maiorem

Dei gloriam

Writer and Editor   Geoffrey Garvey
Typesetting and Graphics LINK Book Development and Production
Printer   Wicklander Printing Corporation

Printed in the United States of America.

5   7   9   10   8   6   4

Ad maiorem

Dei gloriam

• A PUBLIC

Christian Liberty

502 West Euclid Avenue, Arlington Heights, Illinois 60004

Contents

Unit 1: Physics and Chemistry 1

    Focus 2

    Chapter 1: Machines 3

    Chapter 2: Solid, Liquid, Gas 7

    Chapter 3: Things Join to Make New Things 11

    Chapter 4: Metals 14

    Chapter 5: Liquids 17

    Chapter 6: Magnetism 20

    Chapter 7: Fire and Heat 23

    Chapter 8: Electricity 26

Unit 2: Geology and Botany 32

    Focus 34

    Chapter 9: Minerals 35

    Chapter 10: Volcanoes 39

    Chapter 11: Mountains 43

    Chapter 12: River Valleys 46

    Chapter 13: Sediment and Erosion 49

    Chapter 14: Plants Grow 52

    Chapter 15: Plants Like Light 55

    Chapter 16: The Cycles of Life 58

Unit 3: Astronomy and Weather 64

    Focus 66

    Chapter 17: The Sun 67

    Chapter 18: The Earth 71

    Chapter 19: The Stars 75

    Chapter 20: The Moon 78

    Chapter 21: Clouds 81

    Chapter 22: The Seasons 84

    Chapter 23: Weather 87

    Chapter 24: Climate 90

Unit 4: Biology and Health 96

    Focus 98

    Chapter 25: Animal or Not? 99

    Chapter 26: Kinds of Animals 103

    Chapter 27: Mammals and Birds 107

    Chapter 28: Insects 110

    Chapter 29: Fish 113

    Chapter 30: Germs 116

    Chapter 31: Nutrition 119

Answers to Unit Checkouts 124

Unit 1

The Mystery of God's World

This is a beginning book in the sciences. In this book students are given their first exposure to the ways a scientist looks at nature, matter, energy, weather, and the universe at large. We concentrate on hands-on learning. Students will touch and handle, look and prod, feel and hear some of the fascinating objects and creatures in God's marvelously constructed world. There will be some text for you to read with your students, and some pages will give new facts. These are meant to help the young student to understand the hands-on experiences.

Some of the experiments will have risks of spills, and some, especially those around the stove, will require close adult supervision. These are marked with a safety-first emblem. Some will have you rolling up your sleeves to assist young fingers in making things that are a little challenging. Consider these opportunities to model careful work and enjoyment of the activity. If more than one student is participating, they should take turns. In no case should anyone sit and just watch! (A reluctant child may need a few demonstrations of how much fun the activities are before participation becomes willing and eager.)

Field trip suggestions appear at the end of each unit. We have tried to consider all parts of the country in our suggestions, and we hope you find one or two that you can use in every list we present. We suggest that field trips be used as refreshers and rewards on the week of the checkout.

You may complete a whole lesson in one day, or you may do the introductions one day and each "experiment" on the other days, for three short science lessons per week.

Most primary grade children cannot reason with the same agility as adults can. Reasoning requires practice and "muscle building" in very much the same way as physical skills. A logical connection that you can see without effort may seem no more plausible to your young student than a fairy-tale answer.

If a question proves challenging, the student must at least **try** to reason out the answer, but must not reach the point of frustration and discouragement. The following motto may help you know when enough is enough: The question should prove to the child that he **can** think and get an answer, and not seem to prove to him that he **can't.** Suggest the correct answer **before** the point of frustration is reached and check for understanding, then move on whether understanding is achieved or not. At this age, the factual knowledge is not the primary learning goal.

God put the world into our care with the commands of Gen. 1:28–29. Our caretaking responsibility requires at least three ingredients: to love God's world, to believe we are empowered to take care of it, and to have the hope that we are equipped to do so. These three ingredients come with our faith, and it is our hope that this little book will provide opportunities for your students to develop that love, to strengthen that belief, and to broaden that hope.

A child's wonder at the marvels around us open our adult eyes to the fact that God really has made a marvelous world. As the Lord says (Mt. 18:3), "Verily I say unto you, Except ye be converted, and become as little children, ye shall not enter into the kingdom of heaven."

In Christian fellowship,
Dr. Paul Lindstrom

"In the beginning, God created the heaven and the earth. And the earth was without form, and void. . . . And God said, Let there be light, and there was light."
—Gen. 1: 1–3

Focus

Here are some pictures of things in the world God made. God wants us to use the gifts He gave us. Some of the things on this page are not as God made them. They were built by people to make our world a better place to live. Color the things that people made from God's gifts red. Color the things that are the way God made them green.

Instructions: Children at this age often lack the experience to tell what comes directly from nature and what has been manufactured. Expect some questions and some instructive mistakes. Learning without correction is superficial; at the same time, correction should be done with Christ-like humility.

Some children may know that people sometimes build lakes. If the lake is colored green, simply make sure that the student knows that most lakes are made by God! Be sure to emphasize that even man-made things are possible only because God provides man with the appropriate wisdom and resources.

A machine is something that makes work easier. Not all of them have motors. In fact, some do not move by themselves! We might think of some of them as tools.

A car **is not** a simple machine. It is a machine made of many smaller machines. A seesaw **is** a simple machine. A small child can bounce a larger child or even an adult by sitting on the longer end.

One thing in each row makes work easier. Circle them. A scientist would call these things machines. Cross out the things that do not make work easier.

1.		ROCK		WAGON
2.		SCREWDRIVER		TREE
3.		BARBELL		CROWBAR
4.		SEESAW		SHIRT
5.		WHEEL		COIN

4

Learning about God's World

Do you ever have to pull a wagon or pedal a riding toy up a hill? Is it easier or harder than when the ground is level and flat? Is it easier going up or coming down? Does it matter how steep it is?

Are there any wheelchair ramps at the corners near your house? Have you ever seen wheelchair ramps at the entrances to public buildings or churches? Why are ramps easier than stairs for wheelchairs?

You need:
- A bicycle (tricycles and most riding toys will be too wide)
- An outdoor staircase
- A board 1" by 6" and at least 6 feet long
- A box of books weighing 5 to 10 pounds (just light enough for a student to lift, but too heavy to hold for very long)

Set one end of the board on the first step. Push the bicycle up the board. How hard is it? Now put one end of the board on the top step. Now try pushing the bicycle. Is it harder or easier?

Can you push the bicycle up the board from the bottom to the top step? Now stand at the bottom of the steps and look up to the top steps. Can you **lift** a bicycle that high?

Now push the box of books up the ramp. Can you make it all the way? Could you lift the box that high?

The fact to be experienced is that a ramp (an inclined plane) makes work easier. The details of how and how much are not important at this age. See if you can lead your student to statements like "it's easier with a ramp" or "ramps help you do work."

Learning about God's World

One simple machine is used to weigh things. Let's build one and see how it works.

You need:
- A (12-inch) ruler
- A wire hanger with a cardboard tube for a bottom
- A knife
- About 24 inches of string in two equal pieces
- Two men's handkerchiefs of the same size
- A place to hang the hanger where it can swing free (a chandelier or a broom over the backs of two chairs)
- Lots of pennies (20 will do, but the more the better)

Use the ruler to find the center of the cardboard. Get an adult's help to make a very small cut (no more than 1/4 inch) at the center. Mark the center "C." Then make cuts 1, 2, 3, and 4 inches from the center cut. Be careful not to cut too far into the tube or it may bend or break!

6

Tie one end of each string around the four corners of each handkerchief. Just the corners! The sides should hang open a little so you can get pennies in and out. Tie the other end of each string in a loose loop around the cardboard tube of the hanger. You want to be able to move the handkerchief bags back and forth easily on the tube.

Set the bags at one inch from the center. Hang the hanger where it can swing free and check the balance. Does it balance straight? Put ten pennies in each handkerchief and check again. Move both loops to the center and check again. The balance can be fixed by changing the shape of the hanger. An adult will have to do this hard part.

Put both bags way at the ends. Put one penny in one of the bags. That side of the ruler should now go down. The penny makes it heavier.

Now put two pennies in the other bag. Now **that** side goes down. Two pennies is heavier than one penny.

Let's try this: Move the two pennies 1 inch from the center. Does the side with the two pennies go up? Why?

Let's find out some more about how this works. Put ten pennies in one bag 1 inch from the center and three pennies at the 4-inch mark. What if you move them to the 3-inch mark?

This "scale" will not be very precise, but it will provide a good start on one of the basic ideas of mechanics. Try several combinations with your child until at least this much becomes clear: The same number of pennies at the same distance balance; a different number of pennies at the same distance do not balance; and the same number of pennies at a different distance do not balance. See if your student can, unassisted, say in some way that the farther from the center a weight is, the stronger the pull it makes on the "balance." Students who find this activity fun may discover that some "unequal" combinations balance: 2 pennies at 1 inch balance 1 penny at 2 inches; 5 pennies at 4 inches balance 10 pennies at 2 inches. Some of these students may instinctively choose balancing combinations: weight times distance on one side balances weight times distance on the other side. A knowledge of multiplication is not always necessary to see this fact. **Do not strive** for this sophisticated observation, but if it happens, praise it matter-of-factly and move along.

God made the things of the world in three forms, solid, liquid, and gas. A solid is something that keeps its shape. A block of wood is a solid. So is a rock. So is a nail. Solids do not drip or flow through a pipe.

A liquid is something between a solid and a gas. It does not keep its shape, but it stays mostly together, and it forms an edge. Water is a good example of a liquid.

A gas has no shape at all and will try to fill up whatever it is in—sideways and up and down. Air is a gas—really, many gases all mixed together. Air fills up a whole room from wall to wall and ceiling to floor. It is funny that we call gasoline "gas" for short. It is really a liquid like water, isn't it?

Circle the liquids. Color the solids brown.

8

Learning about God's World

safety first

You need:
- tea kettle or saucepan
- water
- cookie sheet

Try this. Boil some water in a tea kettle. (No tea kettle? A saucepan will work almost as well.)

Hold a cookie sheet over the steam. Did you get water drops on the bottom of the cookie sheet? Did it "rain" from your cookie sheet?

Explanation: Steam is just water that is heated until it becomes a gas. The water must be hot enough to turn to steam (212°F). The cookie sheet is much cooler than that. The cookie sheet cools the steam and changes it back to water.

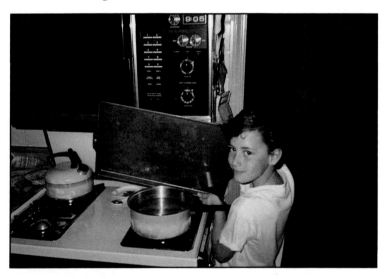

Learning about God's World

You need:
- two jars less than 4 inches high
- bathtub (or sink)

You are going to pour air into a jar. First fill the bathtub with 6 inches of water. (The sink will work, but the tub is a little easier.) Dip one jar in the water until it is full.

Keep the jar completely under the water as you turn it upside down. Lift the jar of water halfway out of the water. The water will stay in the jar as long as the top is under water.

Keep the other jar straight upside down and put it under the water. If it is straight and you move it slowly and gently, no water will come into it.

Now move the jar of air underneath the jar of water. Tilt the jar of air so the air goes up into the jar of water. The jar of water will fill with air.

You have just poured air into a jar!

Things can change from solid to liquid to gas. Heat can cause this change.

Ice is solid water. Water flowing from the faucet is a liquid. And if you boil water, it changes to steam, a gas. If you boil a pot of water long enough, all the water changes to steam. Do you think it disappears?

Chapter 3

Things Join to Make New Things

Things can mix together. When things just mix, both things are still there. Some things mix so well that one thing seems to disappear. We call that kind of mixing **dissolving.**

Things can join, too. When they join, though, a new thing is made. It can be very hard to get back what you started with!

Some things don't mix at all.

You need:
- 1/2 cup of raw rice
- yellow and red food coloring
- two jars or glasses, 6 ounces or larger

Let's make a picture of what dissolving is like. Put two tablespoons of the rice in a jar. Put three or four drops of yellow food coloring on the rice and stir. Keep stirring until all the rice is yellow. Measure two tablespoons of rice into the other jar or glass and color it red. (If you put in a lot of food coloring by mistake, wait for it to dry.)

Pour the red rice into the yellow rice and shake it up. The red and yellow rice got mixed all through each other, didn't they? Pour the rice out on a sheet of newspaper. Can you separate the red from the yellow? You might need a lot of patience, but you see that you can do it if you want to.

Now let's make a picture of joining. (Scientists call this a **compound** or a **chemical change.**) Pour the rest of the uncolored rice into one of the jars or glasses. In a teaspoon, put a few drops of red and a few drops of yellow food coloring. Mix the colors together. Now drip the color from the teaspoon onto the uncolored rice. Stir it until all the rice is colored.

Can you separate the red grains from the yellow grains now? Right, there are no red or yellow grains. They are all orange.

Learning about God's World

You need:
- 4 glasses
- 2 paper cups
- 3 spoons
- vinegar
- sand
- sugar
- baking soda
- fine strainer
- large bowl (2½ qt or larger)
- water

Let's try three things. Get three glasses. Fill two glasses half full with water. Fill the third glass half full with vinegar. Put the glass with vinegar inside a large bowl. There are going to be spills.

Put a half spoonful of sand into the first glass of water. Stir it for a while. Then leave it alone. What happens?

Put a half spoonful of sugar into the second glass of water. Stir it for a while. Then leave it alone. What happens?

Put a half spoonful of baking soda into the glass with vinegar. What happens? It will bubble very hard. After it stops, stir it gently for a while.

These are some differences you should see. All the sand should be down at the bottom of its glass. (Is it really all?) Most of the sugar, or maybe all of it, will seem to be gone. (Where?) The baking soda and vinegar went crazy. Something strange happened there. (What?)

Stir the first glass with sand again and quickly pour the mixture through the strainer into a fourth glass. Measure the sand in the strainer. It should be about the same as you put in (a half spoonful).

Empty the strainer, pour out the water from the fourth glass, and rinse the strainer clean. Now take the second glass and pour the water with sugar through the strainer into the fourth glass. How much sugar do you see? Measure it. Where is the rest?

Empty the glass and rinse the strainer again. Now pour the vinegar and baking soda solution from the third glass through the strainer. How much baking soda do you see? There should not be a trace of anything.

The sand and water made a **simple mixture**. The sugar **dissolved** in the water. The baking soda and vinegar joined to make a new thing—actually a few new things. One of the new things was a gas that made all those bubbles. This was a **chemical change**.

Chapter 4
Metals

Metals are a special kind of thing. They are so special and useful that there are some scientists who spend their whole lives studying them. There are a large number of metals in the world, and some are right around you.

Do you have any coins in your pocket? Those are made of metal.

Look under the kitchen sink. Do you see metal pipes there? One of them is probably very hot, because it carries hot water to the faucet. (Some homes now have plastic pipes.)

Are there pots and pans in the kitchen cabinet? They will be all metal or mostly metal unless they were made for the microwave.

Here are some special things about metals that make them useful.

- They carry heat well.

- Most of them carry electricity well, especially gold, silver, and copper, but also steel and aluminum.

- They can be softened by high heat without burning or changing to a liquid. This makes them easy to shape.

- They can be stretched and pressed into shape by big machines.

- They can be polished until they are very, very shiny.

Learning about God's World

You need:
- bowl of boiling water
- a metal spoon
- a wooden ruler or a pencil
- a whole piece of chalk

Have an adult boil some water and pour it into a bowl. Hold one end of the chalk and put the other into the hot water—just the end! Wait 5 seconds. Do you feel anything at your end?

Now do the same thing with the pencil or ruler. Do you feel anything after 5 seconds?

Now try the spoon. Did you even have to wait 5 seconds to feel something?

Learning about God's World

Let's see how shiny we can make things.

You need:
- two rocks
- two pieces of plastic
- two pieces of wood
- two smooth pieces of metal that aren't rusted (old tin cans are all right if they have no sharp edges anywhere)

Rub the two rocks together. What happened? Probably one left a white mark on the other.

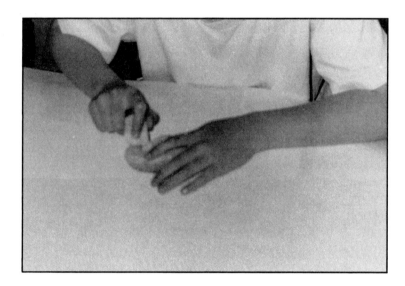

Rub the pieces of plastic and the pieces of wood. Did anything get shinier? (Sometimes the wood will get a little shinier.)

Rub the pieces of metal. Do they get shinier the more you rub? All metals can be polished this way.

On our earth we can usually tell liquids from gases by a very simple test. We are used to thinking that a liquid is something we can pour from a pitcher into a glass, or from one glass into another. When you are older, you may learn that it is not so simple! Maybe you thought of saying that sugar can be poured—is sugar a liquid? (Of course not!)

For now, let's say that a solid forms **pieces,** a liquid **has an edge that can move** or forms **drops,** and a gas tries to spread out as much as it can.

Learning about God's World

You need:

- two small glasses or jars
- water
- cooking oil

Take two small glasses or jars you can see through. Get the smallest ones you can find, as long as you can put your finger in them easily without getting stuck. Pour some water in one of them until it is not quite full. Pour some cooking oil in the other to the same height.

Now let's try some things with the oil and water. First tap the surfaces. (The surface is the top edge of something.) Do not dunk your finger under the surface—tap firmly, but without going through the surface. Watch carefully how the surfaces act. Do both surfaces seem to bounce up and down, almost like gelatin?

Wait until they stop bouncing and look at the **shapes** of the surfaces. Do you see how the water surface curves up at the edges? You probably see less curving in the oil, or maybe none at all.

There are some unusual liquids that curve the **opposite** way on their surfaces. One such liquid is the silvery liquid in thermometers called **mercury.**

Now have an adult fill the glasses or jars as full as they can go without spilling. (This should be done somewhere where messes are easy to clean.) Which one can be filled past the top of the glass? Don't answer too fast—look! Which one filled higher? Why did this happen?

Learning about God's World

Now let's see just how strong the surface of a liquid is.

> **You need:**
> - water
> - cooking oil
> - waxed paper
> - toothpicks

Get out a piece of waxed paper. (Cellophane and plastic will not work nearly so well.) Put some drops of water and oil on the waxed paper.

Take two toothpicks, one for water and one for oil. Break off the end of the one for the oil so you do not get mixed up.

You should be able to tell which is oil and which is water by the color. The oil should look yellowish. The water should be colorless. Can you tell?

Take the water toothpick in your hand. Find a water drop. If you can be gentle enough, and if the drop is not too big, you can **drag** a water drop around the waxed paper with the toothpick. Find two water drops close together. Can you drag a water drop with the toothpick until it hits another water drop? What happens then?

Take the oil toothpick in your hand. Try the same things. Do the oil drops act like the water drops? How are they the same? (It is not enough to say they are both drops! Think!)

The oil and water are alike because they are both liquids. You could not push two blocks of wood or two rocks together the way you can push two drops of water or oil together. And gases do not make drops.

Which one makes bigger drops, the water or the oil? The one that makes bigger drops has the stronger surface. Remember when the glass or jar was filled past the top? Did the one that filled up higher also make bigger drops?

Scatter a small amount of salt or sugar on your waxed paper. Take another toothpick and try to do with the grains what you did with the water and oil. Is salt a liquid? Is sugar a liquid?

Take a really close look at a grain of sugar or salt. Really, really close. Does it look like a drop? If your eyes are really good, maybe you can see that they look like a baby's blocks. Can you see the corners and the edges?

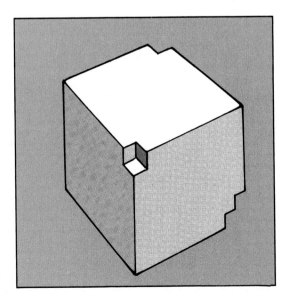

Chapter 6

Magnetism

Does your refrigerator have magnets stuck to it? What is a magnet? Why does it stick to the refrigerator but not your bedroom wall?

Does your family have a portable checker or chess set? Will the pieces stick to a cardboard checkerboard?

Learning about God's World

You need:

- a camping lantern battery
- a piece of iron about 6″ long and less than 1″ thick
- a piece of electric wire about 7 feet long
- some needles and pins
- a permanent magnet (any shape)

The wire must be the kind that has plastic around it. Wind the wire around the piece of iron at least twenty times. Leave about 12″ of wire at both ends for attaching to the battery.

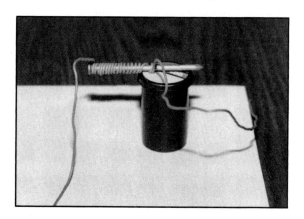
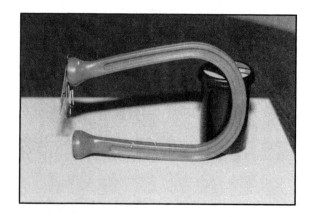

When you are done, attach one end of the wire to one side of the battery.

Put some needles and pins about 1" from one end of the piece of iron. Does anything happen? Leave the needles and pins and the piece of iron where they lie. Attach the other end of the wire to the other side of the battery. Does anything happen now?

Let's see if the piece of iron turned into a magnet. With one wire off the battery, hold the iron near the pile of needles and pins. Anything? Attach the wire again. What now? Take one wire off the battery again.

Pick one needle from your pile. Hold it over the pile of needles and pins. Does anything happen?

Connect your electric magnet and hang the needle from one end of it. Move the needle close to the pile of needles and pins. What happens?

Did the needle turn into a magnet? Let's check. Disconnect the magnet again. Hold the needle over the pile again. What happened?

Is it the electricity? Let's check. Get a permanent magnet. Hang your needle from this magnet. Move the needle close to the pile again. Now what happens?

Iron and steel are a little special. They turn into magnets when a magnet touches them or is near enough to them. When the magnet goes away, they stop acting like magnets.

Let's Make a Permanent Magnet

Get a good steel needle. Turn on your electric magnet. You are going to rub the needle on one end of the magnet, but listen first and make sure you understand how to rub. The rubbing is a little tricky.

First we need to pick a direction on the needle. Let's say we will start by the eye and work toward the point.

When we rub, we will touch the end by the eye first. Then we will rub by pulling the needle along the end of the iron. The last part of the needle to touch the magnet will be the point.

Then we will lift the needle and not let it touch the magnet. We will bring the eye of the needle back over the magnet. Then we will touch the eye end to the magnet and rub toward the point again. Can you count to 50? Do this fifty times.

The more you rub, the better your needle magnet will be. The more carefully you rub in one direction only, the stronger your needle magnet will be. The stronger the magnet you rub with, the stronger your new magnet will be.

Check it out. Does your needle magnet pick up pins by itself now?

Chapter 7
Fire and Heat

Fire

Many of God's gifts can be used wisely or foolishly—for good or evil. Fire is one such gift. We must always remember to be careful with it. If we build a fire in a safe way and in a safe place, the fire will give us heat and light. The heat keeps us warm and healthy. When there is no daylight, the light of a fire lets us see the work God has given us to do.

If we carelessly build a fire in a dangerous place, or forget to be careful with it, the fire can hurt us or burn up what is precious to us.

Is there a fire in your home right now? You may say, "We do not have a fireplace." Well, what keeps your house warm in the winter?

Probably, there is a heater or a furnace of some kind, somewhere in your house. Certain kinds of furnaces burn oil. Some burn coal. Others burn natural gas (not gasoline, but a true gas as opposed to a solid or liquid). And some run on electricity. Electric furnaces work like big toasters to keep your house nice and toasty warm.

If you have electric heat, you are right to say, "We do not have a fire in our home." (Of course, we also must be careful with electric heat. It too can cause fires.) We will look at electricity in the next chapter.

Fires need three things to burn: fuel, heat, and a certain kind of fresh air. Take away one of these things and the fire will go out.

You may have seen a fire burn itself out by using up all the wood (or fuel) in a fireplace. Have you ever blown out a candle? If so, you moved the fire away from its fuel, and it went out.

We put out many fires with water, cooling the fire and removing the air.

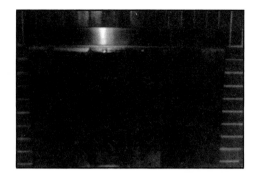

Learning about God's World

You need:
- some candles with holders
- a glass (not a plastic one—it may melt or catch fire!)
- matches with an adult to light them

safety first

Let's put out a fire by taking away its air. Light a few candles, as the boy in the picture has. Hold the glass two or three inches above one flame. (Hold the glass too low, it will get hot. Hold the glass too high, you will have a long wait.) While you watch, the flame will get lower and go out.

Now move the glass slowly and carefully, keeping it straight upside down, over another burning candle. Did this candle go out faster? Then move the glass over a third candle and try the same thing. Faster again?

Did you ever put your head under your bed covers a long time, until it was hard to breathe? You used up all the fresh air. The candle just did the same thing. It used up all the fresh air in the glass.

Check it out. Turn the glass right side up and swing it around a little to fill it with fresh air. Put it over another lighted candle. Did it take longer, like the first time again? It should.

Heat

You need:
- saucepan, 2 to 4 quarts
- 1 or 2 quarts of water
- glass soda pop bottle, 12 or 16 ounces (empty)
- balloon

Fire gives us heat. A pan on the stove becomes hot when the very tiny parts of the pan become very excited and begin moving very fast. How can the pan stay together? Well, that is something about solids. (Remember solids, liquids, and gases?) In a solid, the tiny parts stay in one place, but they can move back and forth a little way.

Try this. Fill a medium-sized pan half full with water and set it on the stove to boil. Meanwhile put a balloon over the top of a soda pop bottle.

Set the bottle in the hot water. What happens?

The balloon begins to fill because the air inside the bottle moves around so much that it pushes against the balloon and stretches it. Put the bottle in the refrigerator for a while and watch the balloon shrink back again.

There are three kinds of electricity.

One kind comes from a battery. It is called **direct current.** We usually use direct current only for small pieces of equipment. Flashlights run on direct current from batteries. Some radios can run on direct current from batteries. Larger pieces of equipment like refrigerators would need very big batteries!

The second kind is called **alternating current.** It runs our refrigerators and powers our lights. Some radios plug into the wall outlet and run on alternating current. Some radios can run either on batteries or on house current. Alternating current is very much like direct current. It comes into our houses through heavy wires that we can see on utility poles in our neighborhood.

Direct current and alternating current both flow along wires. Both can light up a light bulb.

 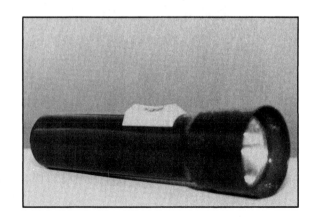

The third kind is called **static electricity.** It is very different from the other two. Nothing runs on static electricity. It does not flow along wires. It cannot light up a light bulb. It is the kind that makes "static cling" that you may have seen on television commercials, where they show clothes that stick together.

Learning about God's World

You need:
- a balloon
- a piece of fuzzy cloth (a sweater will do nicely)

Static electricity can make things behave like magnets. Let's look at some of them. Stand near a wall. Rub the balloon on the cloth a few times. Quickly touch the balloon to the wall and gently let go. Did it stick? If not, try it again. (This works best in dry weather, or in the winter.)

Stand near a mirror and rub the balloon on the cloth. Look in the mirror. Now hold the balloon over your head. What happens to your hair?

Is there a really dark closet in your house? Take the balloon and cloth into the closet and watch closely when you rub. Did you see sparks? What color were they?

The color may actually be any of several colors. It will help develop the student's powers of observation to be given this specific question.

Learning about God's World

You need:
- two lengths of insulated copper wire, each about 12″ long
- two large steel nails
- an orange, possibly two or three
- a small flashlight bulb

Stick the two nails into opposite ends of the orange. Strip an inch of insulation from the ends of both wires and wrap one end of each around a nail. Wrap the unattached end of one wire around the light metal sleeve at the base of the flashlight bulb. Touch the end of the other wire to the dot on the bottom of the bulb. Do you see a faint glow?

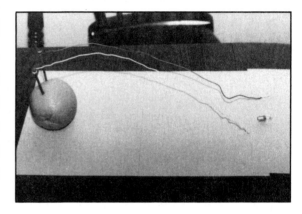

No glow? Try a darker room. (There is not a lot of current here.) Still none? Connect a series of oranges like this:

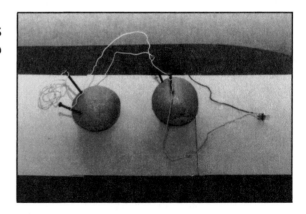

You will not need to empty the refrigerator to get enough current to light the bulb.

Field Trips

- Earth-moving equipment at a large construction site nearby can give your student an opportunity to see how some of the simple machines are put to use: a steam shovel uses a combination of a pulley and a lever; a bulldozer's shovel is a wedge.
- If there is a person known to your child who is wheelchair-bound, or if you can locate such a person willing to take the time, you may arrange for your student to interview the person about the difference a ramp makes at corners and at building entrances. The personal application of mechanical principles can make the lesson memorable.
- A water purification plant, dam, or reservoir in your area may be equipped to give public tours. The points to look for and the questions to ask would be those that concern how the flow of water is controlled and the problems water flow presents for the work.
- A gas supplier could be an instructive visit for your student. Not all owners would welcome the interruption, and their receptiveness may depend on how busy the season is when you telephone. If a foreman at the shop can talk about the problems of handling a gas, the experience will be especially memorable.
- At oil refineries, the sludgy liquid petroleum is heated and separated into gasoline, kerosene, paraffin, and so on in tall cracking towers. The lighter gases are piped off higher up. A tour may not be a practical possibility, but nearly as much may be learned by a good long look from the road as from an inside tour.
- Mercury, being both a metal and a liquid, has a unique usefulness: silent electrical switches can be made with it. Being a metal, mercury conducts electricity very well; being a liquid, mercury can flow away from two bare ends of wires inside the switch so that electricity can't pass between them. (Air is a very poor conductor of electricity.) Mercury switches are not as widely available as they once were, but a long-established hardware or electrical-goods store nearby may have one your students may see.
- Your local electric utility may provide tours of its electric generating plant or at least allow a visit so that your students may see how electricity is produced. With luck, they may have some informational brochures written at your students' level. If the generating plant is near to you, in it you may observe how a magnet is spun past wires to generate electricity. Your student may learn in a memorable way about the caution one must have around electricity and may begin to develop an appreciation for electricity as a valuable gift.
- A visit to a fire station is always an experience that students find exciting. Fire fighters are usually glad to explain to young people what their work is and can explain many facts about water pressure in the hose, the properties of various kinds of fires, and how different kinds of fires are controlled and extinguished.

Unit 1 Review

With each fill-in, follow this procedure: (1) read each sentence twice with the answer; (2) tell the student to listen for your pause and say the word that belongs; (3) read the sentence again and pause instead of saying the **boldface** word in red. The student is to say the word that completes the sentence correctly.

1. A machine is something that makes work **easier.**

2. I have a scale that balances. If I move the weight on one side farther from the center, that side will go **down.**

3. Water is a **liquid,** and ice is a **solid.**

4. A liquid will turn to a gas if it is **heated.**

5. When salt **dissolves** in water, we can get the salt back by drying up the water.

6. When two things join to make a new thing, we call that a **chemical change.**

7. Gold is a **metal.**

8. Two things that metals do well are **carry heat** and **carry electricity.**

9. One thing a liquid has that a gas does not have is **a surface.**

10. A metal that is a liquid is **mercury.**

11. A magnet will not pick up **plastic.**

12. The needle on a compass is a **magnet.**

13. To burn, fire needs **air, heat,** and **fuel.**

14. Heat will make the tiny parts of a pan **move back and forth.**

15. The three kinds of electricity are **direct current, alternating current,** and **static electricity.**

16. A dangerous form of static electricity is **lightning.**

Unit 1 Checkout

Answer the questions.

1. Name something that a magnet will not pick up.

2. Name two things a fire needs to burn.

3. Name one thing that metals do well.

Fill in the blanks.

4. I have a scale that balances. If I move the weight on one side closer to the center, that side will go _____.

5. The three kinds of electricity are direct current, alternating current, and _____.

6. One thing a liquid has that a gas does not have is _____.

7. A machine is something that _____.

8. A liquid will turn to a _____ if it is heated.

9. The needle on a compass is a _____.

10. Water is a liquid, and ice is a _____.

11. A dangerous form of static electricity is _____.

Circle **Yes** or **No**.

12. A metal that is a liquid is mercury.	**Yes**	**No**
13. When salt dissolves in water, we can get the salt back by drying up the water.	**Yes**	**No**
14. When two things join to make a new thing, we call that dissolving.	**Yes**	**No**
15. Gold is a metal.	**Yes**	**No**
16. Heat will make the tiny parts of a pan fly apart.	**Yes**	**No**

Assist the student with the reading and writing, but leave the student free to choose answers alone. Decline to supply answers kindly. The answers are on page 124.

Unit 2

The Beauty of God's World

In unit 2 the student will explore the creatures of the third day of creation, the dry land and the plants. The earth and its features and some basic concepts of the life of plants will be covered. The student will also learn basic differences between living and nonliving things. The important concepts of the water cycle and the carbon cycle will also be presented.

The main concepts that the student should grasp by the end of the unit are:

- Mineral products that we use every day
- The internal structure of the earth
- What a volcano is
- How mountains are formed
- How an earthquake happens
- Some properties of rivers
- How the earth's water is distributed
- The importance of topsoil as a resource for human beings
- Basic facts about erosion and how erosion is controlled
- The main differences between living and nonliving things
- The importance of plants in the food chain and in the earth's oxygen supply
- Phototropism (the growth of plants toward the sun)
- The importance of sunlight in the photosynthetic process of plants
- How the water cycle functions

You may want to take a moment to review how the learning has progressed to this point. Was the unit review sufficient for the student to recall the material that had been covered in the lessons? If the student missed several questions or it seems that the student merely memorized the answers in the unit review and is still a bit uncertain about the concepts behind the words, consider introducing more frequent reviews. You may quickly go over the material at the end of each lesson before continuing to the next. Sometimes the time lag between lessons presents a problem for the student: if lessons have been presented once a week, consider presenting the lesson in two or three stages on separate days. Some students may benefit from reviews after two or three lessons instead of waiting until the end of chapter 16 in this unit.

Pay attention to your student's interest as you progress through the material. If your student's interest in one topic is high, take a little extra time. Think about encouraging an interest that may blossom into a career at a later age.

"And God said, Let the waters under the heaven be gathered together unto one place, and let the dry land appear; and it was so. . . . And God said, Let the earth bring forth grass, the herb yielding seed, and the fruit tree yielding fruit after his kind."
—Gen. 1: 9, 11

34

Focus

Plants, earth, water. Earth, water, plants. Water, plants, earth. God made these three things to work together. Each helps the other do its work in God's plan. While they work, they produce our food and our beautiful earthly home.

Color the plants green. Color the earth brown. Color the water blue.

Chapter 9
Minerals

When God made the earth, he didn't make it all of one kind of thing. Think of all the things that are on the land.

There is sand. There is the rich, dark soil that we can grow food on. There are rocks.

There is more than one kind of sand. Some sand is almost white. Some sand is yellowish. There is even some sand that is black—and not because it's dirty!

There is more than one kind of soil. Some is dark and spongy and breaks apart easily in our hands. Some is heavy and sticky and we can make a ball out of it. Some is dry and crumbly.

There is more than one kind of rock. Some rocks are shiny and have sharp points. Some are smooth. Some look flaky like a pie crust.

God knew that we would learn to make things for ourselves, and He put many things we could use in the land. He left them there for us to find and learn how to use.

We get all our metals from rocks: iron for buildings, cars, and bicycles; aluminum for cars, bicycles, and soda pop cans; gold for computer and phone parts and jewelry.

Many things we use every day come almost straight from the earth (after they are cleaned): most baby powder is a kind of crushed rock; salt is from the earth; the "lead" in your pencil comes from a rock that is like coal; one mineral makes biscuits rise.

Many plastics, fuels, clothes, and medicines come from oil that we find in the ground.

Here are some products we use every day that are minerals from the earth:

Rocks come in many colors and shapes. Some people spend their whole lives learning about rocks: where the different kinds can be found, how they formed, and what they tell us about the earth.

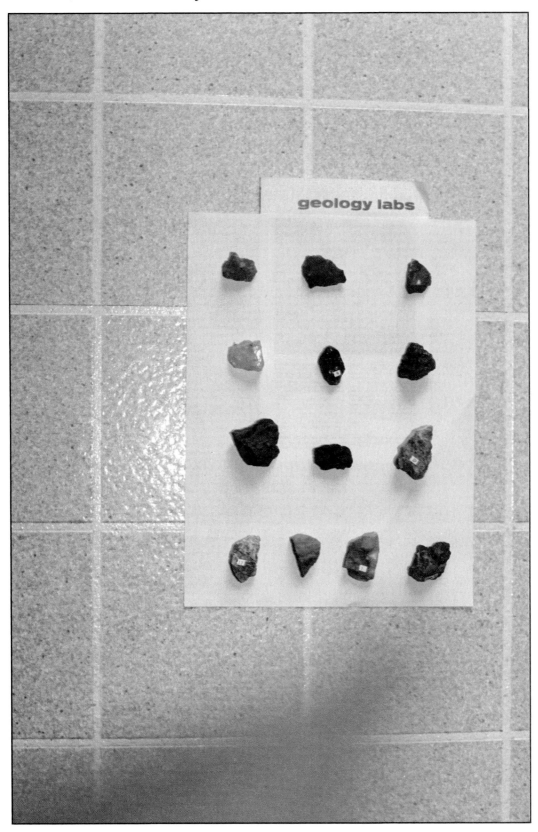

Learning about God's World

You need:
- a penny (3)
- a pocketknife (5)
- a piece of glass or old mirror (6)
- a steel file (7)

Here is a way to test rocks for hardness. The numbers in the list above tell how hard each object is. These numbers are based on the **Mohs'** scale which you should look up in a dictionary or an encyclopedia. You may count your fingernail as a number two (2) on this scale.

A harder thing will scratch a softer thing. However, a scratch does not count if it is just a white smudge that rubs off. For example, if you scratch a rock with a penny or a pocketknife, and it does not leave a permanent mark like the piece of glass, then the rock would score a number 6. Therefore, we can give a number to any rock we find by testing it against our five objects. Always start with your fingernail and go up the scale until you can make a permanent mark with one of the five objects.

The missing numbers (1, 4, 8, 9, and 10) are things that are hard to find at home. In case you find these rocks at a rock shop or souvenir stand, you will be able to complete your collection: 1 is talc (the rock–not the baby powder made from it); 4 is fluorite; 8 is topaz; 9 is corundum; 10 is diamond.

Collect at least ten different kinds of rocks and test them for hardness. Identify as many rocks as possible. The library is the best place to find books that will help you name them. Perhaps you could visit a local museum (or university) that has a geological section which displays various types of rocks. Record your finding on this chart or make one of your own.

No.	Rock	Score	No.	Rock	Score
1			9		
2			10		
3			11		
4			12		
5			13		
6			14		
7			15		
8					

Remember solids, liquids, and gases? Do you remember that things can change from solid to liquid to gas? We saw that ice can change to water when it warms and water can be heated to turn into a gas form, steam.

Every solid can change to a liquid and a gas. Even rock.

You know that things can be cool on the outside while they are still hot inside. Think of a fresh french fry, straight from the fryer. The outside can be cool enough to touch. It can be cool enough to put in your mouth. Then you bite it, and ouch! Hot!

The earth is like that. It is very hot inside, and besides, it isn't hard all the way through. Hot, melted rock flows many miles below the surface. Where the surface of the earth has cracks, the melted rock can rise to the surface.

Melted rock coming up through the cracks makes a volcano. You may have heard the short name we use for "melted rock": lava.

Have you seen cracks in the ground when the weather is dry? Don't worry! The cracks have to be hundreds of miles deep to start a volcano.

Of course rock that is hot enough to be a liquid is hot enough to turn water and other liquids to gases. Do you think that happens in a volcano? Of course it does! Water and other liquids that are under the earth become very hot from the melted rock in the volcano, and those liquids change to steam and other gases.

Volcano Eruptions

Gases bubble up through the lava, and the lava can sputter and splatter and splash as it spews out of the volcano. The lava can splash hundreds of feet into the air, especially if the volcano is partially blocked.

Try this in a sink. Turn on the water. Put your finger or thumb partially over the spout on the faucet. The water will travel farther and faster. (Watch out for splashes!) The tighter you put your thumb over the spout, the harder the water flows.

This is how it is with a volcano. Sometimes the lava just flows out the spout, called a **cone.** Sometimes the cone is a little blocked, and the gases sputter the lava a little into the air. Sometimes the cone is mostly blocked, or maybe there is a lot of gas trying to get out, or maybe the lava is very thick. Then the lava really sputters and shoots high into the air. Sometimes the cone is very blocked and there is a lot of gas trying to get out. Then the volcano might throw huge chunks of rock and globs of lava very high into the air.

Learning about God's World

You need:
- baking soda
- flour
- water
- vinegar or lemon juice
- lots of modeling clay (at least one pound, or four sticks)
- red and yellow food coloring
- chopstick, ballpoint pen, or thin twig

We cannot make a real volcano. But we can build something that looks and acts like one. Find a place that can get messy for this project. For the simplest volcano, mold the clay into a volcano shape. Shape it into a peak like a mountain. Then push a hole into the top with your thumbs, maybe 2 or 3″ deep.

Put two tablespoons of baking soda into the hole. Mix three drops of red food coloring and one drop of yellow with the baking soda until it is all orange. Then quickly pour a quarter glass of vinegar or lemon juice into the hole. The foam will flow down the "volcano" sides like lava.

We can make the kind of volcano that sputters, too. (This doesn't always work.) Make sure the inside of your volcano is empty and dry. Then put two or three tablespoons of baking soda in it. Color it as before and pack it down well.

In a small glass, mix one teaspoon of flour with a half teaspoon of water (or less) to make a thick paste. Spread the paste over the baking soda. Spread the paste evenly and try to cover all the baking soda. The paste should not be very thick.

Shove the chopstick, pen, or twig through the paste and almost all the way through the baking soda. Let the paste dry a day or two.

When the paste is crusty, carefully remove the chopstick, pen, or twig. There should be a hole in the paste that stays open. This narrow hole is our partially blocked cone. Now pour a quarter or a half glass of vinegar or lemon juice into the hole.

If the vinegar or lemon juice can get deep enough into the baking soda, your volcano should break open the paste cover, or at least ooze around it with some force.

There are a few ways that mountains are made. New mountains can be made at any time.

Do you remember that the earth is not hard all the way through? There's more. The surface of the earth (called the **crust**) has big cracks in it, and pieces of the crust are floating around on the liquid rock. (Not very fast. North America is drifting toward Asia at a speed of a few inches a year.)

There is a mountain-building project on page 44. The books are two moving pieces of the earth's crust. Sometimes pieces of the earth's crust push together and something folds between them, making a mountain range like the fold in the newspaper.

Other mountains are made when one piece of the crust rises up and over another piece, like the two books alone on page 44.

Sometimes two pieces of the crust just slide apart. Maybe one slides north and up and the other slides south and down. The higher piece makes the mountain.

What holds these pieces lopsided like that? Good question. The answer is "Not much." This is what's called a **fault** in the earth's crust. The pieces could slide again, making an earthquake.

Learning about God's World

You need:
- newspaper section, four to six sheets thick
- two books
- one helper

Some mountains are made this way: Take a section of newspaper, at least four sheets thick. Open it flat on the floor, with the crease in the middle. The newspaper will be a flat prairie. Each of you take a book to a different side of the "prairie." Set each book against the edge of the newspaper. Slowly, each of you slide the books a few inches toward each other.

Did the prairie get a mountain range? Was it along the crease?

Here's another way mountains are made. Bring just the books together. Put them back to back. Very, very slowly (don't ruin the books!) push the backs of the books together. If you push slowly, the back of one book will rise up over the back of the other by an inch or so.

You can try making mountains from sheets of clay in place of the newspaper and books. Keep the sheets of clay nice and thick so they make nice thick bends.

Learning about God's World

You need:
- some ground where you are allowed to dig (the beach is a good choice)
- grubby clothes
- a bucket of water
- a dipper
- a shovel

Make a big pile of earth and sand, as high as your patience will let you. Pack it down good and hard with your hands and the shovel. Don't make too sharp a point at the top.

With the dipper, dribble a little water on the top of the mountain. Dribble, don't pour! You're trying to be rain, not a flood! The water will start to flow down the mountainside. Watch the water flow. Watch the shapes it makes.

Dribble some more. Watch the river get deeper and wider. It will work its way further down the mountain.

If you have the patience, make two or three mountains very near each other. Dribble little rivers down each of them and see if they join to make a bigger river.

Many rivers start in mountains. Here's how. First remember that water always goes as low as it can.

It rains or snows on top of the mountain.

The rain runs down, or else the snow melts and runs down. Water likes to get low.

The stream of water passes around all the bumps and high spots. Water likes to stay low.

The stream is joined by other streams running down the mountain. The streams join to make a creek, then a river.

The water digs into the earth, making a stream bed or riverbed. This makes a path for the next flow of water to follow.

Learning about God's World

You need:
- bathtub
- 48-oz. (1½-qt.) juice bottle or pitcher
- 16-oz. container (large frozen juice can, extra-large coffee mug, large individual soda-pop bottle, etc.)
- 12-oz. container (frozen juice can, normal coffee mug, soft-drink can, etc.)
- 4-oz. juice glass
- tablespoon

Assemble the listed materials before the lesson. We cannot stress enough the importance of (1) having the measuring go smoothly, without interruption, and (2) having one individual container to represent each place that water is.

All children at this age are very concrete, from the brightest to the slowest. To use a container twice, to fill an overly large container partway, or other variations, risk turning this concrete visualization into an abstract concept and thus losing the student's interest or compromising the student's understanding.

If your student happens to think of rain and clouds, all atmospheric water together could be represented by a large (10 oz.) tumbler.

Fill your bathtub with about 4 inches of water. This stands for all the water in the world.

Take the juice bottle or pitcher and fill it from the tub. This is how much water stays frozen as snow or ice in the cold parts of the world and on tops of mountains. Set the "frozen" water on a table and label it FROZEN.

Take the largest container you have left and fill it full from the tub. This is water that sits or flows underground. (Wells bring this water to the surface for us to use.) Set it next to the ice-and-snow water. Label it UNDERGROUND.

Take the largest container left and fill it from the tub. This is how much water there is in all the lakes of the world. Label it LAKES and set it next to the underground water.

Now fill the juice glass from the tub. This is the water that has been soaked up by all the soil in the world. Set it on the table and label it SOIL WATER.

Fill the tablespoon from the tub. Now what's left in the tub is—the water in the oceans! What's in your tablespoon is all the water in all the rivers and streams all over the world!

Where Do Rivers Go?

Rivers, of course, are headed for the lowest place they can reach. For many rivers, the end is the sea. For a few others, the end is a lake. Many rivers join other rivers before either reaches the end.

There are nine rivers in the United States more than 1,000 miles long.[1] Five of them flow into the sea. Three of the others flow into the Mississippi, one of the first five. The ninth, the Snake, flows into the Columbia, another of the first five.

Only one river in the United States more than 350 miles long ends in a lake: The Red River of the North, which flows from Minnesota to Lake Winnipeg in Manitoba, Canada.

From rivers comes water for farming, especially when there is not enough rain. As we will learn in the next chapter, rivers are important to farming for other reasons, too.

What is really important about rivers, though, is their place in God's plan for water in the world. In God's plan, no water is ever wasted.

1. Water flows through the rivers to the oceans and lakes.

2. It **evaporates** from the oceans, lakes, and rivers like the water from the tea kettle we saw on page 8. It also rises from our breath and the breath of animals. (Have you seen the little cloud coming from your mouth on cold days?) Even plants put water into the air from their leaves.

3. The water, in gas form, rises through the air until it gathers in clouds.

4. Rain and snow fall from the clouds and water the earth, making rivers and nourishing the plants.

5. Water flows through the rivers to the oceans and lakes again.

---

1. We present the nine U.S. rivers longer than 1,000 miles (in order of length) in case you feel your student is in need of memorization practice: Mississippi, Missouri,* Yukon, Rio Grande, Arkansas,* Colorado, Red,* Columbia, Snake.* (Those with asterisks flow into other rivers.) The names may be written on a chalkboard and repeated with the student until the student can, unassisted, name them all in order without looking.

Chapter 13

Sediment and Erosion

One thing that rivers do is the best thing that ever happened to farmers and the worst thing that ever happened to farmers.

First you should know that the best soil for growing plants is called **topsoil.** You will probably not be surprised to hear that topsoil is the soil on top of the ground.

In some very fertile places of the Ohio River Valley (Illinois, Indiana, Kentucky, and Ohio) the topsoil can be 18 inches deep. Some areas have half an inch or less of topsoil.

Topsoil comes from dead plants, either from grassland or from forests. Farmers can put some fertilizer in the ground where there is not enough topsoil, but fertilizer is expensive. It is usually not worth while to spend a lot of money on fertilizer unless your crop pays extremely well.

Another problem that sometimes comes from chemical fertilizers is that the ground becomes very hard. This makes a new problem.

A farmer is better off starting from good land.

It sometimes happens that rivers help farmers. In Egypt there is a river called the Nile that used to flood every year. The farmers were very glad because this river carried topsoil from the jungle, where no one needed it. After the water went down, the farms along the river were very good for growing crops. They had fresh topsoil every year.

But most of the time, farmers worry about water carrying away the good topsoil they have.

Learning about God's World

You need:
- an empty planter or large box (18 × 36″ or larger)
- a thick plastic sheet at least as large as the box
- three rubber balls or other round objects 2 or 3″ in diameter
- soil
- a plant sprayer or clean hair sprayer with plain water
- a watering can
- grass seed
- a stick about ¼″ thick

Place the three balls in the box under the plastic sheet. Space out the balls until they are at least 8 inches apart. Spread out the plastic sheet to completely cover the bottom and sides of the box.

Pack some soil over and around the "hills" made by the balls. When the soil is packed well, get the stick ready. You're going to do some farming.

Leave one hill alone. This is cleared land the farmer is going to ignore. On the middle hill, plow some lines up and down the hill with the stick. Go straight from the bottom to the top, not so hard that you go all the way to the plastic.

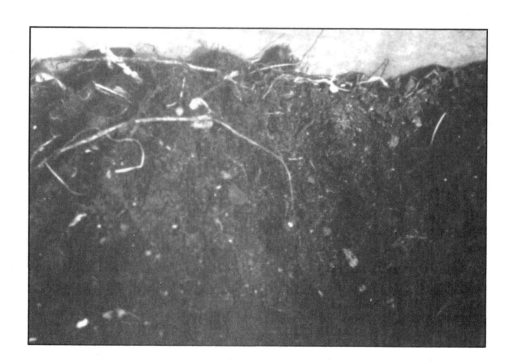

On the last hill, plow in circles around the hill. Make one circle near the bottom. Make another halfway up. Make a third circle almost at the top.

Plant the two plowed hills with grass seed. Put the seed close together, but all in the furrow. Spray the ground to moisten it. Keep it moist for several days until the grass grows.

When the grass is well grown, make a heavy rain with the watering can. What happens to the soil?

There should be heavy erosion on the bare "hill." (Look for the student to use a word that suggests the concept of erosion. The word itself may be too difficult to remember.) The "hill" with vertical "furrows" will probably show erosion between the rows of grass. The third hill should show the least erosion. There may be some terracing build up of soil uphill from the "furrows."

Farmers control erosion by plowing around hills, instead of up and down. This is like the plowing we did on page 50. Farmers also try not to leave ground bare. Plants help hold the soil down, especially on hills. Trees help keep the wind from blowing topsoil away.

River Deltas

When a river ends at a lake or an ocean, the water might slow down quite a bit. Water won't carry as much soil when it runs slow. Rivers drop some of their soil at their ends.

Some of the dropped soil might be carried by the ocean a little bit away from the river. The dropped soil builds out farther and farther into the sea. In a long time, a delta might grow hundreds of miles long and hundreds of miles wide.

Sometimes the river gets blocked with soil. Then the river flows around the block and cuts a new path. The same thing happens again and again.

When this happens, the end of the river can have many paths. The river might spread out in a kind of fan. The fan is full of topsoil the river dropped, and this land is sometimes very rich for farming.

The formation of river deltas is greatly simplified here, almost to the point of inaccuracy. Not only have we omitted some of the complexity for the sake of clarity, but scientists themselves do not understand everything about how river deltas occur. Here is a task for scientists of the future.

Did you ever think about the difference between a plant and a rock? It may be silly, but it is an important question.

The difference between a plant and a rock is the difference between a living thing and a nonliving thing. To understand the difference is to begin to understand God's precious gift of life.

Here are some differences:

1. A plant can make more plants like itself. A rock cannot make more rocks like itself. (Breaking into pieces does not count.)

2. A plant uses food and makes the food into part of itself. A rock does not use food.

3. A plant grows and changes without turning into something else. A rock cannot become larger or change without becoming a different rock.

4. A plant has a time when it first begins to grow and use food and a time when it no longer grows or uses food. These are the beginning and end of its **life.** There are not such clear beginnings and ends in the existence of rocks.

Plants are also important because all life on earth depends on them in very many ways. Plants are like factories that make all of the food we eat and all of the air we breathe. If most of the plants on earth died, all humans beings would probably be dead in less than a year.

(However, that many plants are not ever really likely to die all at once.)

Learning about God's World

You need:
- 10 dried beans—lima, pinto, black, red, kidney, mung, soy, blackeyed peas, cowpeas, crowders, or whatever is handy
- 10 paper cups, 4 oz. or larger
- paper toweling
- plastic bags or plastic wrap
- soil and water

First soak the beans overnight. Wet the paper toweling and fold it over once or twice. Then place the soaked beans on the paper toweling and fold the toweling over the beans to protect them from light. Cover the toweling with plastic wrap or set the toweling in a plastic bag. This will help keep the beans moist.

Fill each paper cup not quite full with soil.

Every day, make sure the paper toweling is wet and check the beans for growth. In a few days you should see a sprout splitting the bean. Carefully put the bean just under the top of the soil in one paper cup. Water the soil until it is damp but not soupy. Label the cup with the day and a letter from A to J (a different letter for each plant).

Put the cup in the sun and keep the soil moist. Once your bean plants break through the ground, measure the growth and keep a little chart:

Day	Bean Plant Heights									
	A	B	C	D	E	F	G	H	I	J
1										
2										
3										
4										
5										
6										
7										
8										
9										
10										

Plants Are the Beginning of All Food

Here is a funny story about a scientist who wanted to find out how much soil a tree needed to grow.

This scientist was a very careful person. Everything was set up very carefully. There was exactly 400 pounds of dirt, not a speck more or less, in a big barrel. The barrel weighed exactly 30 pounds. The acorn the scientist planted weighed ½ ounce.

The scientist was careful not to let any new dirt get into the soil, not even fertilizer—and not even **liquid** fertilizer. The scientist watered the tree every day and made careful notes on the height of the tree. He came to like his tree and began to be proud of its beauty.

When the tree reached a certain height, the scientist moved the barrel with the tree to a big scale and weighed it. He knew he started with 430 pounds and half an ounce. Now he had a puzzle, because the tree, barrel, and dirt now weighed 600 pounds! Well, maybe he put a lot of water in that barrel today when he watered it—but that is a lot of water!

The scientist weighed a pail of water like the one he had been using and started keeping track of how much water he added.

Years later, the tree and barrel and soil weighed 1,000 pounds. Now the scientist was really wondering! He took the tree out of the barrel and weighed everything separately. The tree weighed 570 pounds by itself! The barrel still weighed 30 pounds. The amount of water the scientist had added? 300 pounds. So if everything adds up, the tree used 240 pounds of dirt.

How much soil did the tree use for food? It weighed 399¾ pounds—only ¼ pound less than at the start! More than 239 pounds of tree seemed to come from nowhere! The scientist gave up. He figured either he was a bad scientist or trees grew by magic!

What the scientist did not know was that trees grow by using water, air, and sunlight. Very little soil is needed, except for a place to send out roots. Animals cannot live on air, water, and sunlight. Neither can we. We must eat something. The plants are the food factories of the world.

Save the bean plants grown in this lesson for use in chapter 15.

Chapter 15
Plants Like Light

In chapter 14, you learned that plants make food from sunlight, water, and air. In this chapter we will look at plants and sunlight.

You may have noticed two plants that show very much how they like the sun. One likes the sun so much that its name says so: the sunflower. Are there sunflowers growing in your yard or a yard nearby? Some day watch them follow the sun through the day.

Morning glories decorate many front yard fences. If you know where some grow, check them sometime on a cloudy day and again on a sunny day. Or check them in the daytime and again near sundown. You will see how they open when the sun shines and close tightly when there is little or no sun.

Learning about God's World

You need:
- the 10 bean plants (or however many have survived) from chapter 14
- black construction paper
- masking tape
- a clear windowsill in the sunlight (southern exposure if possible)

Set half the bean plants on the windowsill. Put the rest of the plants in a dark place, maybe a closet if no carelessly tossed shoe or toy will spill them. Leave the plants alone for a week.

After a week, put the plants together. Can you tell which is which? The plants that grew in the dark should be paler, taller, and weaker-looking.

- They are paler because plants need sunlight to turn green.
- They are taller because plants are built to stretch after the sun.
- They are weaker-looking because a plant cannot be healthy without sunlight.

Put all the plants on the windowsill. Notice where the sunlight lands on the plants. Block the sunlight partially with the black paper. Tape the black paper in place. Do not move the plants or the paper for a week.

After a week, check the plants. Have they grown like this?

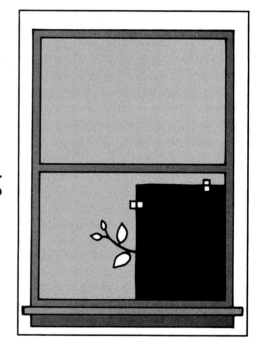

Automatic Light-Seeking Device

Plants, of course, do not have brains. How do they know how to grow toward light?

The fact is, without a brain plants cannot "know" anything. God has made plants automatic, so they don't need brains. Let's build something to find out how God's automatic light-seeking device works.

You need:
- wire or rubber tube 6″ long and ¼″ thick
- wire or rubber tube 8″ long and ¼″ thick

(Any two very flexible objects ¼ to ½″ thick, one of which is approximately one-third again as long as the other, will serve the purpose. Use wire or tubing that is green if possible.)

Plants are made of tiny parts called **cells.** Our two sizes of tubes or wires will stand for plant cells.

The first thing you should know is that God has made plant cells to grow more when they are in the dark. Plant cells that are in the light grow normally.

The second thing you should know is that plant cells are all attached together, almost like glued, the top of one to the bottom of the next, and the side of one to the side of the next.

Take the long tube or wire. This stands for a plant cell that was on the dark side of a plant. It grew more because it was in the dark. Take the shorter tube or wire and line up one end with the other tube or wire. Tie those ends together **tightly.** Remember, plants cells are all attached.

But the plant cells are attached at the top, too! Tie the tops together. Now what happens when you bring the top ends together?

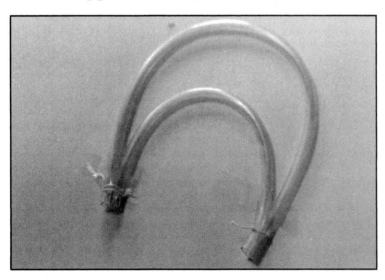

Which way did the tubes bend? Toward the shorter tube? And the shorter tube was on which side, the light side or the dark side? So the tubes bent toward which side, the light side or the dark side?

Do you see how God's automatic light-seeking device works?

Some students may need a more concrete demonstration. There is no shame in this. Turn on a light and mark the "light-side cell" in some way, with marker or paint. Keep that side toward the light. Emphasize that the bottom of the tubes start out at the same time and are attached together. They stay attached all along the one side where they touch. And they are attached at the top. So when the "dark-side cell" grows longer than the other cell, both have to bend to stay attached.

Chapter 16

The Cycles of Life

Do you know the word **cycle**? You have seen and heard it in **tricycle, bicycle, unicycle,** and maybe **cyclone.** It means "circle" or "wheel." A cyclone turns in a circle. A **uni**cycle has one wheel, a **bi**cycle two, a **tri**cycle three. (We might call a car a quadricycle.)

There are two important circles in God's creation, and we call them cycles. The first one we will talk about is the water cycle, or how water circles through creation. The second is called the carbon cycle.

Water Cycle

The amount of water that evaporates into the air is exactly the amount of water that falls back to earth as rain or snow. The fact may seem simple and obvious, but think about it. It wouldn't have to be so.

- The water from rain and snow could just keep sinking further and further into the earth until it stayed there and there were no more clouds in the sky. Or maybe not all of it. Maybe **just a little** each year until the clouds were all gone.

- The water that evaporated could all keep rising on out of the atmosphere and disappear into space. Or again, maybe not all of it. Maybe just a little until it was all gone.

- Maybe the living things on earth could hold in themselves more and more water until no more reached the clouds. Until the clouds disappeared.

But none of these things happens. All the water that evaporates, sooner or later falls as rain or snow—every drop. And all the water that falls to earth returns to the clouds—every drop.

Here is more. Not all the water that falls on the land comes from the land. Almost one-third of it evaporated from the ocean. So the ocean ends up lending the land some of its water. Again, it would not have had to be that way. It could just as well have been the other way: that more water evaporated from the land than fell on the land.

There is still more. It could be that the oceans eventually dried up from lending the land so much water. But that does not happen either! First the land's plants are watered and thirsty animals get water to drink. Then every drop of water that came from the ocean returns to the ocean, either from rivers or under the ground.

It's all perfect. Now who could have planned that but God?

Carbon Cycle

Something called carbon goes around in a circle, too. This circle is not as tight and perfect as the water cycle, but then it does not need to be.

All food on earth starts with plants. Part of the air is a gas called **carbon dioxide** (CAR-bun dye-**OX**-hide). Plants use energy from sunlight to take the carbon from carbon dioxide. Plants join the carbon with water and other gases from the air to make things we and the animals need in our food: protein (PRO-teen), carbohydrates (CAR-bow-**HIGH**-drates), fat, and vitamins. After taking carbon from carbon dioxide, oxygen is left over, and the plant breathes it out into the air.

An animal breathes the oxygen from the plant and eats the food the plant makes. Now the animal joins these things into new things too, manure and carbon dioxide. The manure will fertilize the land for new plants. And then the carbon dioxide is in the air for the plants to join with water again using energy from the sun! The animal when it dies will also fertilize the land for plants.

"For as the rain cometh down, and the snow from heaven, and returneth not thither, but watereth the earth, and maketh it bring forth and bud, that it may give seed to the sower, and bread to the eater"—Isaiah 55:10.

Learning about God's World

You need:
- A saucepan with boiling water
- two cookie sheets
- a couple of oven mitts

Do not try to do this demonstration unless one of your parents is in the same room with you. The saucepan with boiling water stands for the **ocean**. The steam from the saucepan represents the moisture that evaporates from the ocean as the sun beats down upon it.

As the water boils, have one person with an oven mitt hold a cookie sheet on the edge of the saucepan. It should be at about a 30° angle (see diagram below). This cookie sheet stands for the **land**.

Next, you should use an oven mitt to hold the second cookie sheet over the saucepan. It should rest on the first cookie sheet at about a 60° angle between the two cookie sheets (see diagram below). This second cookie sheet represents the **clouds** in the sky.

Notice how the steam from the saucepan (ocean) collects on the second cookie sheet (clouds). This cookie sheet is cooler than the steam. The moisture forms droplets of water on the surface of the cookie sheet.

As more moisture collects on the second cookie sheet it will begin to run down onto the first cookie sheet (land). This is like the rain that falls on the ground. Some of the water soaks into the ground, and some of it flows into streams and rivers. Finally, it flows back into the ocean—as the water in the cookie sheet runs back into the saucepan.

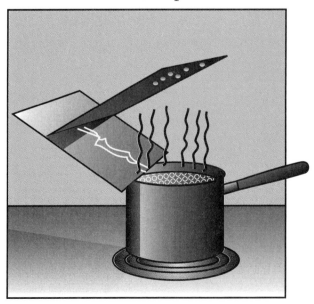

Field Trips

- A mining or ore-processing company can provide a very memorable form of learning about the earth and how it is composed. The problem will be locating the right company to see what you want to see. Some mining companies maintain only a small office that manages affairs for a group of investors and speculators, and there will be nothing relevant to learn in such a place. On the other hand, even if the location near you does not actually process ore, it may be staffed with a public relations department eager to provide information and it may have instructive brochures within the reach of your student's understanding.

- A visit to a river can be a good first-hand lesson for a young student. If there is a river source nearby, all the better. There are few better ways to understand what a river is than to see one at its source. A planned canoe trip or camping trip can be the occasion of a science lesson as well. In any river visit for this purpose, point out to the student how the water has dug its channel into the ground. Show where the current flows fastest and where it eddies behind rocks, fallen logs, etc. Point out the different plants that grow **in** the river, **along** the river, and **away from** the river.

- It will not be possible on most mountains to see the rock folding, since soil usually has buried the evidence. Some highways, however, have cut through rock layers and it is possible to see the folding. The geology de-partment of a university near you will certainly have suggestions on good sites to see rock folding from mountain formation in your area.

- A gorge or river canyon is an excellent place to see rock layers. Of course, everyone knows the Grand Canyon, but there are many smaller canyons that are just as instructive to see and at the same time more accessible. Again, telephone the geology department of a nearby university for suggestions. (Gorges and canyons are more common in the states west of the Mississippi.)

- There are a few arboretums scattered through the United States, places where native trees are grown and protected. If you are lucky enough to have one nearby, they can make a most instructive visit and a pleasant family walk besides.

- Botanic gardens are pleasant and instructive places to see plant life. If there is one near you, make plans for a visit.

- Trees are grown commercially in tree nurseries, and state and national forests and logging areas will have areas where young trees have been planted. Permission will be necessary to visit a private area such as a logging plantation or a tree nursery, and explanations in such visits may be brief, but if there are no public forests nearby you may find them better than nothing.

- A greenhouse can make a good field trip. Pick a time for a visit when business is slower: November to February or mid-summer. Greenhouse workers can be very informative about plant needs and characteristics when they are not under pressure.

Unit 2 Review

With each fill-in, follow this procedure: (1) read each sentence twice with the answer; (2) tell the student to listen for your pause and say the word that belongs; (3) read the sentence again and pause instead of saying the **boldface** word in red. The student is to say the word that completes the sentence correctly.

1. Four things we get from rocks are **iron, gold, baby powder,** and **salt.**

2. The center of the earth is **very hot.**

3. Hot, melted rock is called **lava.**

4. A volcano starts from **a crack in the earth.**

5. When part of the earth's crust slides over another part, **a mountain** is made.

6. Sliding pieces of the earth's crust can cause **an earthquake.**

7. Rivers begin with **rain and snow in the mountains.**

8. Most of the earth's water is in **the oceans.**

9. The part of the soil that is good for growing crops is called **topsoil.**

10. The washing away of topsoil is called **erosion.**

11. Two things that control erosion are **plants** and **proper plowing.**

12. Two things a living creature does that a nonliving creature does not do are **grow** and **use food.**

13. All food on earth begins in **plants.**

14. A plant left in the dark will **stretch** to find the sun.

15. Plants use sunlight to **make food.**

16. The amount of water that falls to earth and the amount of water that evaporates from earth are **equal.**

17. When a plant makes food from sunlight, it produces a gas called **oxygen.**

Unit 2 Checkout

Answer the questions.

1. Name one thing a living creature does that a nonliving creature does not do.

2. Name two things we get from rocks.

3. Name one thing that controls erosion.

Fill in the blanks.

4. The amount of water that falls to earth and the amount of water that evaporates from earth are _____.

5. Sliding pieces of the earth's crust can cause _____.

6. The washing away of topsoil is called _____.

7. Plants use sunlight to _____.

8. When a plant makes food from sunlight, it produces a gas called _____.

9. Rivers begin with _____.

10. The part of the soil that is good for growing crops is called _____.

11. Hot, melted rock is called _____.

Circle **Yes** or **No.**

12. The center of the earth is very cold.	**Yes**	**No**
13. A volcano starts from a crack in the earth.	**Yes**	**No**
14. When part of the earth's crust slides over another part, a river is made.	**Yes**	**No**
15. Most of the earth's water is in the clouds.	**Yes**	**No**
16. All food on earth begins in oceans.	**Yes**	**No**
17. A plant left in the dark will stretch to find the sun.	**Yes**	**No**

Assist the student with the reading and writing, but leave the student free to choose answers alone. Decline to supply answers kindly. The answers are on page 124.

Unit 3

The Majesty of God's World

In unit 3 the student will review creation on the second and fourth day: the stars, the moon, and the planets in the heavens and the "waters above the firmament"—in other words, the weather.

The main concepts for the student to grasp in this unit are

- That there are nine planets in the solar system and that the earth is the third planet from the sun
- The sun's composition and some of its basic properties
- The earth as a planet, and how it moves through space
- What constellations and galaxies are, and what the difference is between them
- That the sun is a star
- The size of the universe
- What makes the phases of the moon
- How a cloud is formed
- The different kinds of clouds
- How the seasons occur
- The protective properties of the atmosphere
- Some ways that weather is studied, and some basic weather terms
- Some factors that influence climate

You may want to take a moment to review how the learning has progressed to this point. Was the unit review sufficient for the student to recall the material that had been covered in the lessons? If the student missed several questions or it seems that the student merely memorized the answers in the unit review and is still a bit uncertain about the concepts behind the words, consider introducing more frequent reviews. You may quickly go over the material at the end of each lesson before continuing to the next. Sometimes the time lag between lessons presents a problem for the student: if lessons have been presented once a week, consider presenting the lesson in two or three stages on separate days. Some students may benefit from reviews after two or three lessons instead of waiting until the end of chapter 24 in this unit.

If your student's interest is high in this unit, you may have a budding astronomer or meteorologist on your hands. Look for ways to encourage the interest if it exists. There is certainly nothing wrong with taking extra time with a lesson if the student wants to explore a topic more thoroughly!

"And God made the firmament, and divided the waters which were under the firmament from the waters which were above the firmament. . . . And God said, Let there be lights in the firmament of the heaven to divide the day from the night; and let them be for signs, and for seasons, and for days, and for years."
—Gen. 1: 7, 14

Focus

God's world is so big, so powerful, and so mysterious that we can be frightened of it. And excited by it. And in love with it. All at the same time. In the next thirty pages or so we will look at things that make many people have these feelings: the universe and the weather.

In Box A, draw something you would wear on a rainy day. In Box B, draw something you would wear on a really hot day. In Box C, draw something you see in the sky at night. In Box D, draw the earth.

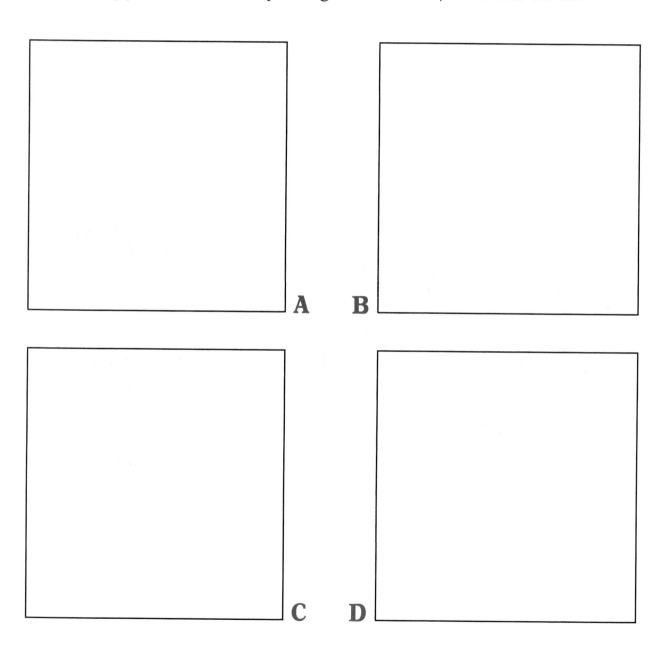

Remember that the purpose of the activity is to focus the student's attention. The drawings may be as humorous, imaginative, or everyday as the student chooses as long as they relate to the topic.

The sun rules the day, as the Bible says. We have already learned that plants need the sun to live. And animals need plants to live. The sun's heat keeps the air on earth warm enough for us all to live. The sun makes all life on earth possible.

The sun is in the middle of a place in the universe we call the **solar system.** The solar system has 9 planets and many smaller objects.

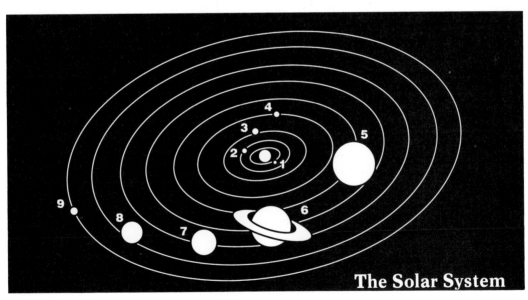

The Solar System

1. Mercury	4. Mars	7. Uranus
2. Venus	5. Jupiter	8. Neptune
3. Earth	6. Saturn	9. Pluto

Mercury and Venus are closer to the sun than we are. They are both too hot for us to live on. Mars is the next planet after us. It is too cold. Only the earth is the right temperature for us. God knew exactly what He was doing when He put man on earth.

Learning about God's World

Did you ever get into a car on a summer day after the car had sat in the sun for an hour? Did the inside of the car get hotter while it sat in the sun? The sun's light is very strong. If we use a magnifying glass to concentrate it, it can start a fire. Let's see what the sun can do.

You need:
- a magnifying glass
- a piece of scrap paper
- a small piece of wood

Pick a sunny day for this experiment. Pick a place where there is no danger of fire spreading—a bare patch of ground or perhaps a metal bucket if there is a lot of dry vegetation around.

Set the piece of paper on the ground. You can use the wood to keep the wind from blowing it away if you need to. Hold the magnifying glass over the paper until you see the sun's light on the paper.

Find the right distance at which to hold the magnifying glass so you make the smallest possible dot of light on the paper. Wait a few moments. What happens?

First the paper will start to smoke, then turn brown. A hole will burn through the paper. Some kinds of paper will catch fire.

Now do the same thing with the wood. If you are careful, you can burn letters into the wood by moving the dot of light slowly. Can you write your name?

Learning about God's World

The sun's light is strong enough to burn paper or wood. It is also strong enough to burn our eyes, so we must be careful. We never, ever look at the sun through a telescope. How can we look at the sun?

You need:
- a thin, stiff piece of cardboard
- a bright, white sheet of paper
- a pin or needle

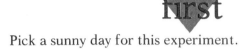

Pick a sunny day for this experiment.

Get a grownup's help to poke a small, clean hole through the cardboard. Hold the cardboard over the paper the way you did with the magnifying glass. Find the right distance so that a tiny clear picture of the sun appears on the paper. You know you have the right distance when you see little gray spots on the sun's picture.

Can you even see the flames shooting from the edge of the sun? You will not be sure you are seeing them right at first. At first you will think your eyes are playing tricks. There really are flame-like things shooting from the sun!

The gray spots you see are cooler places on the sun. They are not very cool, though. The biggest nuclear bomb would be cooler than these cool places on the sun!

The "flames" shooting from the sun are part of its **corona.** Gases from the sun are lit up brightly like fireworks every minute of every day.

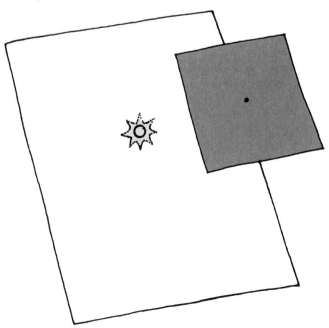

Life from the Sun

Most of the sun is made of the very lightest gas there is, **hydrogen.** Hydrogen is even lighter than the helium that makes balloons float.

The sun is so hot that anything within a few thousand miles of it would burn up instantly. At that temperature, of course, there are no solids or liquids, only gases. On the sun are some things besides hydrogen—even iron. But all things are gases on the sun.

The sun is 93 million miles away from us. (Actually a little closer in winter and farther in summer. We will study this a little in chapter 22.) Even after traveling so far, the sun's light is still strong enough to warm the earth.

We have studied how all food begins with plants. Plants make food from sunlight, air, and water. Plants could not make anything without the sun. It is God's plan to give life on earth through sunlight.

The Sun's Place in Space

Earth is the third planet from the sun. (Look at the diagram on page 67.) The earth takes one year to go around the sun once. In fact, it is the earth's trip around the sun that makes our yearly time period.

The sun is one star in a large group of stars called a **galaxy.** (We will study more about galaxies in chapter 19.) The name of the galaxy in which our sun is, is the Milky Way. The Milky Way is such a crowded patch of stars in the sky because they are so close to us.

Of course, "close" in the universe is not the same as "close" in our neighborhood! The closest other galaxy is the Andromeda Nebula, which is about 12 quintillion miles away. That's

$$12,000,000,000,000,000,000,$$

or, if you could drive 55 miles in an hour to the Andromeda Nebula, it would take you 2½ trillion years to arrive.

God has made quite a large universe!

We can compare the parts of the earth to those of an orange:

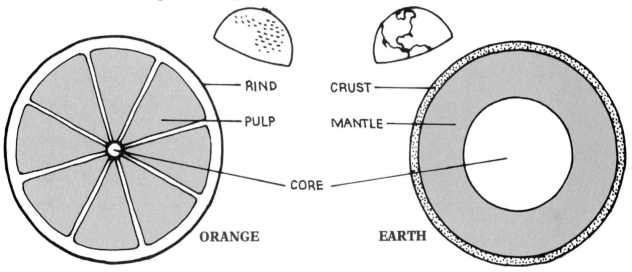

RIND

PULP

CORE

ORANGE

CRUST

MANTLE

EARTH

Air

We sometimes forget that the air is part of the earth because we can't see it. We breathe it all the time, and it is never **not** there. Air is the most important part of our home planet, and not just for breathing:

1. Air protects us from the strongest rays of the sun

2. Air keeps in moisture that might otherwise disappear into space

3. Air moves moisture and plant seeds around, allows birds and insects to fly, and gets rid of poisons a little bit

4. Air holds the sun's heat in

Even if all human beings, animals, and insects wore oxygen tanks, life on earth would be impossible without air.

Learning about God's World

What makes the sun seem to go around the earth? Let's find out.

You need:
- a floor or table lamp
- a basketball or beach ball

Turn on the lamp. The lamp stands for the sun. Hold the ball a few feet away from the lamp. The ball stands for the earth.

Look at the lighted side of the ball. This is daytime on the ball. Look at the darker side of the ball. This is nighttime on the ball.

Stand on the night side of the ball. Keep your head behind the ball. Can you see the "sun"? Move your head to peek around the ball where the hole is. Stop when you can just see the light. Do you see the dawn?

Find the hole on the ball where air goes in. Pretend the hole is where you live on the earth. Turn the hole to the light. Now it is daytime where you live.

Now slowly turn the hole away from the light. Stop when the hole is at the line made by the light. Hold the ball there. Now it is sunset where you live.

Keep turning the ball until it is nighttime where you live.

The earth turns around the way you turned the ball. In some places it is night. In some places it is day. In some places it is dawn, and in some places it is sunset. As the earth turns, daylight comes to new places and sunset comes to other places.

Day starts in the east. When dawn comes to New York, in the eastern United States, it is still dark in California, Alaska, and Hawaii in the west. Three hours after dawn comes to New York, dawn comes to California. Two hours later dawn will come to Hawaii and western Alaska.

Now turn the hole way up near the top of the ball, but on the light side. Turn the ball so that the hole stays in one place while the ball turns. Most of the ball will move from day to night to day to night. What happens at the hole? Is it ever night there?

Think about that. In a few chapters we will talk about it again.

74

Water

Most of the earth's surface is under water. In fact, all of the earth's land surface would fit into the Pacific Ocean with plenty of ocean left over. There are five oceans: Pacific, Atlantic, Indian, Arctic, and Antarctic. There are also many other very large bodies of water in the world. If all the earth's surface were a dollar, the water would be almost three quarters and the land about a quarter and a nickel.

Mantle

The mantle is made of hot, soupy rock. It starts 5 to 25 miles below the surface. All the earth's surface is floating! (No one has been there, of course. Scientists have learned about the mantle from special instruments.)

Is your basement cooler than your attic? Coal miners know that after you dig down deep enough, the mine starts to get hotter. The earth gets hotter and hotter the deeper you go. You will learn more about these interesting facts when you are older.

The Core

The earth, like a baseball or golf ball, has a core. The earth's core is liquid or mostly liquid and is probably about as hot as the surface of the sun! Scientists think that it is mostly metal and is the reason that compasses point north.

Day and Night

In the sky, it looks as if the sun goes around the earth. For many thousands of years people thought that the sun did go around the earth. Then, after the telescope was invented, people found out two truths. First, they found out that the earth turns around once a day, and that makes the sun, moon, and stars seem to move. Second, they found out that the earth goes around the sun.

From the earth, stars are tiny twinkling dots in the dark sky. If there are street lights near, some stars are too dim to see. Stars seem to be cute, delicate little things. But they are really violently roaring super-furnaces, some awesome enough to make our sun look puny!

Our sun is a middle-sized star. Our sun is about halfway between the brightest star and the dimmest star. Our sun is medium-hot compared to other stars.

When we talk about stars, we have to talk about huge distances, enormous power, and unbelievable heat. The nearest star is about 25 trillion miles away. The light from that star started coming to earth before you could walk or talk, and light travels a thousand times as fast as the fastest airplane. Still, that star is a very close neighbor.

Miles are too small to use when we talk about distances in space. Try to measure your house with grains of rice and you will get the idea. So we measure with a bigger thing, called a **light-year.** A light-year is how far light travels in one year. A light-year is nearly 6 trillion miles.

Scientists are fairly sure that other stars have planets as our sun does. We do not know what those planets are like. Maybe there is another planet like earth out there, maybe hundreds or thousands.

We can make wild guesses like these, but in the end we have to admit that we just do not know.

Kinds of Stars

One thing we do know is that stars come in many sizes and colors. We think that at least some stars go through changes. Some of the things that have been seen in the sky make us think so.

Scientists believe that when stars run out of fuel to burn, they start to swell up and turn red. Bigger stars just explode. After swelling and turning red, stars shrink to a small white ball and slowly cool off.

No one has seen such changes happen, because the changes take many lifetimes. But scientists have seen bursts of energy in the sky, and afterwards a star that was blue or white has become red. Some stars have changed from large red objects to tiny white ones.

Groups of Stars

Groups of stars that seem nearby when we look from earth are called **constellations.** You may know some constellations already, if only by name. The ones that are easiest to spot are Leo (the lion), Orion (the hunter), the Big Dipper, the Little Dipper, and Cassiopeia.

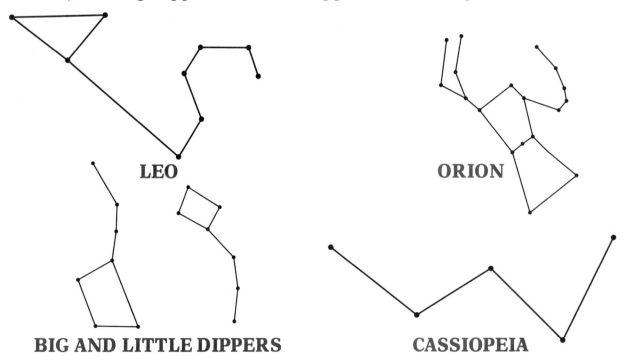

LEO **ORION**

BIG AND LITTLE DIPPERS **CASSIOPEIA**

Groups of stars that really are near each other may form a **galaxy.** "Near" means within a few hundred thousand light-years. The name of our galaxy is the Milky Way. It is shaped somewhat like a pinwheel. Other galaxies are shaped like balls, disks, or eggs.

Learning about God's World

You need:
- A shoe box
- Glue
- Cellophane tape
- Thick black thread or string
- Black marker

- Black construction paper
- Aluminum foil
- Scissors
- Gray plastic screen to cover the shoe box

Cut one of the short ends of the shoe box along the corners, and bend that end down flat. Glue the black construction paper on the inside of the box, including the box top. Draw a triangle with the marker on the plastic screen (3 inches on each side). Place the screen across the top of the shoe box.

Cut four pieces of black thread or string 4 inches long. Cut two pieces of thread 3 inches long. Cut two more threads 2 inches long. Cut one piece 1 inch long. Tie a knot at one end of each string.

This demonstration may be difficult for a young child to understand, but let the student do as much as possible.

The triangle you drew on the plastic screen with the marker should be 3 inches on each side. Draw an "x" at every inch along the sides of this triangle, and place an "x" at each point of the triangle, as in the diagram to the right.

Place the strings through the screen holes, knot end up, at each "x." Squeeze tiny balls of aluminum foil onto the ends of the strings, forming a triangle of balls. Then tape the screen onto the shoe box.

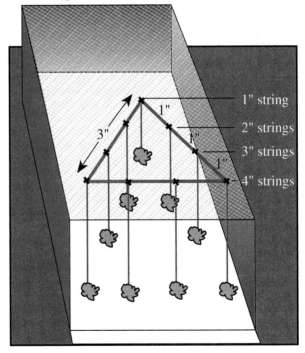

Make one more cut through the back corner of the shoe box (at the uncut end of the box). Place the lid on the box. Look through the open end of the box. Do you see your triangle? Good. Now close that end of your box, and look through the hole that you just cut. Where did your triangle go?

From the earth, we see the stars as if we were looking through one end of a shoe box. However, from another galaxy, we would see the stars as if we were looking through the other end of the shoe box—or even from the top or bottom. We would not see the same patterns in the sky at all.

The moon is the second-brightest object in the sky. Only the sun is brighter. When the moon shines at night, it truly rules the night.

Other planets also have moons. Mars has two. Jupiter has sixteen. Saturn has at least seventeen. (Scientists think they may have missed some.) Uranus has fifteen, Neptune has eight, and even little Pluto has one. But Mercury and Venus have none.

What makes something a moon? Size does not matter much. A few moons are bigger than Pluto, and two are bigger than Mercury. If it goes around the sun, it is a planet. If it goes around a planet, it is a moon.

Sometimes we use **moon** and **satellite** to mean the same thing. A satellite, though, can mean something shot up in a rocket that circles a planet. We would never call such a thing a moon. When we say "the moon" we always mean our moon, the one that circles the earth.

Our moon is very large for a planet of Earth's size. Other moons that big belong to much larger planets.

The moon is made of almost exactly the same things as our earth. This also is strange for a moon. Some scientists have wondered whether the earth and the moon were once a single piece. When God made "the lesser light to rule the night," did He make it from a part of the earth? The Bible does not say He did not, and we do not know for certain.

The moon takes a little less than one month, a little more than four weeks, to go around the earth. The word **month** comes from **moon.** Can you hear it? Can you see it?

Phases

Did you ever notice that the moon changes? Look tonight. Which of these is the closest match?

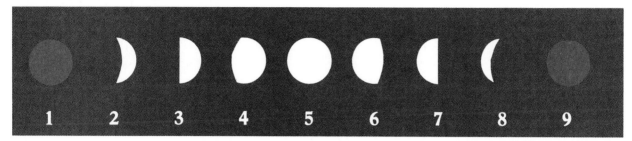

It takes about three days for the moon to change from one of these pictures to the next. In about one week, the moon will change from a thin sliver to nearly full.

The different shapes the moon makes are called **phases.** The phases all have names. These are the names of some of them:

New moon   **1** and **9**
First quarter   **3**
Full   **5**
Last quarter   **7**

Look at pictures 3 and 7. It is hard to remember which comes first. It is hard to remember at phase 3 whether the moon will be full in a week or new in a week. Isn't it?

Here is a way to remember. When you see a C, the moon is **C**losing up. It is getting smaller. If you do not see a C, it is not closing.

Rising and Setting

The sun shines in the day. When does the moon shine? If you answered "at night," think again. Haven't you seen the moon shine in the daytime?

Actually, the moon may rise at any time of day or night. It may rise at the same time as the sun, or just as the sun is setting, or any time in between. The moon will be in the sky about 12 hours and then set.

See if you can imagine this: Moonrise is near sunset when the moon is full. It is near noon when the moon is in its first quarter. Moonrise and sunrise are nearly the same when the moon is new. (If you can not imagine this, use a tennis ball for the moon, a basketball for the earth, and a lamp for the sun.)

Let's Chart the Moon

Make a chart every few days for a month to keep track of the moon's phases. You might also note the rising or setting time. Does a new moon rise at about the same time as sunrise?

MONTH

Day of the Week	Date	Phases
Monday	April 4	First quarter

Chapter 21
Clouds

We saw in chapter 2 that, when water boils, a cloud of steam appears. Is a cloud in the sky the same?

They are really very close to the same. When water boils, some of it turns into a gas. We call the gas **water vapor.** We cannot see water vapor.

Why can we see steam? Because steam is water vapor turned back into tiny drops of water. Clouds are made of tiny drops of water, too. So we can see steam and clouds, but we cannot see the water vapor that becomes steam and clouds.

Here is something special about how clouds happen. Clouds cannot happen in clean air. Water vapor will form the water drops that make clouds only on dust or smoke or something in the air.

Learning about God's World

You need:

- tea kettle with spout
- water

Put one cup of water in the kettle and start it boiling. The heat should be high. Watch the spout closely when it boils. Do you see white steam? Follow the steam down. Is there white puffy steam all the way to the spout? Probably you see a space between the spout and the steam. In this space, the water is still a gas.

Or did you think the steam jumped over a space of air? (Of course it cannot do that!)

God's Pump

Clouds are very important to life on earth. If God had not made clouds and water vapor, life on the land would not be possible.

We learned in chapters 12 and 13 how water runs off the land into the sea.

Suppose we started at the first moment of creation with some clouds. Now say it rains until the clouds are empty. After all the water runs off the land into the sea, won't all the land dry up?

How can water be pumped back from the sea to the land so that plants and animals and people can live on the land?

God built a pump. The water in the sea doesn't need to boil to change to a gas.

Sea water is always **evaporating** and being sucked up by the thirsty air. (Plants send a lot of water vapor into the air through their leaves, too.)

When all the water vapor rises high enough, it turns into tiny water drops. We can see the water drops as clouds.

Then the water returns to the land in the form of rain or snow, and then the rivers carry the water back to the sea. On the way, creatures on the land and the sea receive their share of water.

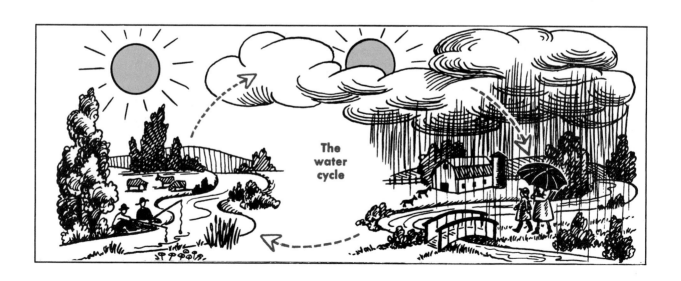

The water cycle

Kinds of Clouds

There are three main shapes of clouds, fluffy, flat, and wispy. Fluffy clouds are called **cumulus** (CUE-mule-us). Flat clouds are called **stratus** (STRAT-us). Wispy clouds are called **cirrus** (SEAR-us).

Cirrus clouds are always very high. Stratus and cumulus clouds can be at many different heights, but they look different at different heights.

When cumulus clouds are high, they may be bumpy near the center and wispy at the edges from the high winds up there. Stratus clouds in the windy heights are thick wisps spread out in strong, straight lines.

When cumulus clouds are at mid-height, much of the sky may be filled with small, cottony bumps, with thick rough bubbles, or a bumpy washboard of clouds. Stratus clouds at mid-height form long, straight streams.

Scientists who study weather can name more than 200 types of clouds. The differences even between these three can be tricky.

Cumulus   **Stratus**   **Cirrus**

Do you know the names of the four seasons? Winter, Spring, Summer, Fall (or maybe in your part of the country you say Autumn).

Did you ever wonder why all the cold weather came together, and all the hot weather together, instead of going back and forth the way rainy days and sunny days can?

The seasons depend on a few things that you have already learned about: the earth going around the sun, the air that surrounds and protects the earth, and the earth turning around to make day and night.

You might think that the seasons depended on how close the earth was to the sun. That has nothing to do with it, as it turns out. In fact, when the earth is closest to the sun, it is full winter in the United States.

There is one more part of it we have not talked about yet. The earth is tilted. About this much:

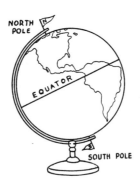

Remember that the air blocks some of the sun's stronger rays. In fact, the air blocks many rays that would make the earth too hot. The more air the sunshine must go through, the less heat the earth receives from the sun.

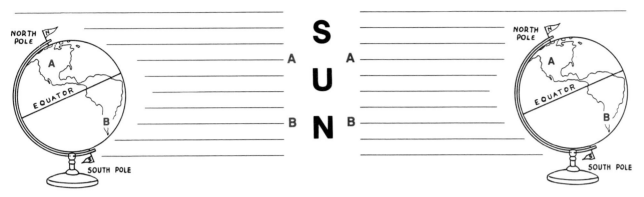

Look at the picture above. Do you see how much air the sun's rays must go through in winter to reach spot B? Measure it along ray A. How much air must the rays go through to reach spot B in summer? Measure it along ray B.

The sun's rays get filtered more in winter than in summer. Our air is like sun screen that people wear to protect themselves from burning in the sun.

There is more, which adds to the effect. The sun spends less time in shining on places that are having winter than in shining on places that are having summer. This may help you to understand:

Learning about God's World

You need:
- lamp
- basketball, beach ball, or globe
- a helper

Make certain that all lights but one are off. This is so you can see the light on the ball or globe better.

with a ball: Have your helper hold the ball with two fingers. His or her fingers should be straight across the ball from each other. Then your helper should tilt the top of the ball away from the lamp.

with a globe: Have your helper hold the globe so that the north pole is tilted away from the lamp. (Most globes are at the correct angle.)

Measure the lit and the dark areas in three places: around the middle (halfway between your helper's fingers), about halfway up from the middle, and about halfway down from the middle.

Write down your measurements in this chart:

Middle (tropics)		Halfway Up (winter)		Halfway Down (summer)	
Light	**Dark**	**Light**	**Dark**	**Light**	**Dark**

Your helper may not have held the ball or globe perfectly steady or perfectly straight. Even so, you should have found that at the middle of the globe the light and dark areas were even or nearly even. The upper portion should have had a dark area larger than the lit area. On the lower portion the lit area should have been larger than the dark area.

The part of the earth that is tilted toward the sun is having summer. The part tilting away is having winter.

Now how do the seasons change?

Move your globe around the lamp, but keep the north pole pointing the same way. Soon neither the top nor the bottom is pointing to the sun. Day and night are about equal all over the earth. The northern half of the earth is having spring. The southern half is having fall.

Keep going around. When you get to the other side, stop and look. Now the northern half is having summer. Do you see it? And the southern half is having winter.

If you measured in each position around the "sun," you would find that at the middle the light and dark areas were always about the same. This area is called the **tropics.** In the tropics there is no summer or winter. The weather is usually very warm in the tropics all year long.

Chapter 23
Weather

If the temperature is 45 degrees in July, is it still summer? If the temperature is 45 degrees in December, is it still winter?

We ask these silly questions to show how easy it is to know the difference between a season and the weather. It is not the cold or heat of one day that makes summer or winter, but how the temperature is for the whole three months.

Weather is what changes from day to day, or even from hour to hour. When we describe the weather we look at things such as

- Temperature
- Moisture in the air
- Wind
- Rain or snow
- Storm activity

In this chapter we will look at some of the things that weather scientists study and how they are studied and described.

You probably already know that temperature is measured with a thermometer. You probably already know what temperature is. Check your knowledge of these temperature facts: water freezes at 32° Fahrenheit (0° Centigrade, or Celsius). 0°F (-15°C) is dangerously cold weather. 100°F (40°C) is dangerously warm weather. Water boils at 212°F or 100°C.

Moisture in the air is called **humidity.** Our bodies have trouble keeping cool in air that is too humid. So hot and humid weather feels more uncomfortable. Hot dry air pulls moisture from our bodies, which means we need more water.

Wind is important in weather for a few reasons. A stiff wind in cold weather can blow the warmth away from our bodies, making it easier for our skin to freeze. Where the wind is coming from may tell us what tomorrow's weather will be like. A hot day with a good breeze may not be so uncomfortable after all. A high wind may be a danger in itself. A heavy snow with a high wind (a **blizzard**) is an extremely dangerous weather condition on foot or in a car.

Clouds may drop their moisture on us in many forms. Have you seen all these? Snow, sleet, hail, rain, drizzle. People usually know what snow is even if they have not seen it in person. Did you know, though, that snow is not simply tiny ice cubes, but fancy, lacy crystals that always have six sides? Fewer people know what sleet is, but it is common throughout the northern United States. It is rain that freezes as it comes down, making very dangerous road conditions and unpleasant walking conditions that are hazardous for older people and others who have trouble walking.

Of course you know that temperature is studied with a thermometer. Do you know the difference between Fahrenheit and Centigrade, or Celsius? On television and radio, temperature is usually reported both in Fahrenheit and in Celsius. Fahrenheit is the older way, but Celsius is 140 years old itself. The United States officially adopted Celsius more than 125 years ago, but many people still feel more comfortable with the older system.

Humidity is measured with an instrument that has a hard name: **hygrometer** (high-GROM-met-er). Weather reports talk about humidity in percent: "The humidity reading is 100 percent" means that the air is holding all the moisture it can.

Wind is measured in miles per hour. Scientists use an instrument a little like a windmill to measure its speed. A **breeze** would name a wind speed up to 12 miles an hour. A scientist would still call a wind of 31 miles an hour a breeze, but you and I would consider wind between 12 and 31 miles an hour a fairly strong wind. (Umbrellas get broken in 31-mile-an-hour winds.) A **gale** is between 32 and 54 miles an hour. People have trouble walking, and trees and roofs are damaged. Faster winds are **wind storms** of one kind or another and cause a great deal of damage.

Rain and snow are measured in inches by catching them in a tube with inches marked on it. An inch of rain is a fair amount of rain anywhere in the country. More than an inch is likely to cause flooding in places that are not prepared to handle it.

Storms that are reported include thunderstorms, blizzards, tornadoes, and hail. These weather conditions are important to report so that people can take steps to keep themselves safe and protect their property.

Learning about God's World

The best way to develop an interest in the weather, and understand what weather study is about, is to do a little. In the chart below, record the temperature, the moisture in the air, the wind speed, the amount of rain or snow, and any storm activity. Get as much information as you can at home with instruments you have there. Get any other information you need from the newspaper or from weather reports.

Date	Temperature	Humidity	Wind Speed	Rain or Snow	Storm?

Chapter 24
Climate

Weather is the temperature, wind, clouds, and so on that can change from day to day or hour to hour. A season is a three-month period of similar weather. What is left that we can call climate?

Climate is how the weather always is in a place, or how it is for many years. Many different things are a part of climate. We can look at rain and snow and notice that Olympia, Washington, has 164 rainy days and 50 inches of rain in an average year, while Las Vegas, Nevada, has only 26 rainy days and 4 inches of rain a year.

We can look at temperature and notice that in an average year Cleveland is cooler in July than Honolulu is in January.

These are a part of the story of climate. Why do people study climate? Climate tells us how easy or hard it is to live in a place, what kinds of things grow there, what kinds of animals can live there, and many other important things.

For example: Some food will not grow in some places because the weather won't stay warm long enough. Some vegetables would rot if they grew in a place with too much rain. Some places are too expensive to live in because people need to make a lot of heat to stay warm. Do you see how climate affects us?

There are dry climates, like the desert, and wet climates, like the jungle. There are cold climates, like the North and South Poles, and hot climates, like southern California and Arizona, the Gulf shores of Texas, and Florida. Some places are windier than others. In some places winter is much colder than summer and in some places the difference is not great.

Climates depend on:

- How strong the sun's rays are

- What kind of land is near

- What the air is like

- What kind of water is near

Sun

A lot of the earth's heat comes from sunshine. This is probably no big surprise. Do you remember this fact from chapter 22?: The sun heats best when it shines straight down. The sun shines down straightest for the longest time over the middle of the earth. Therefore, the warmest part of the earth is the middle, which we call the **tropics.**

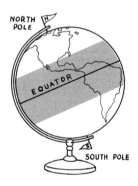

Land Shapes

The shape of the land is important for climate, too. In the 48 mainland states of the United States, winds mainly come from the west. Weather moves from west to east, blown by the wind.

Rain clouds often start in the Pacific Ocean. The western side of mountains in the western United States is often rainy. The eastern side of these mountains often contains dry desert. Hawaii also has many mountains. On the side where the wind usually blows, the climate is rainy. Across the mountain from the rainy side is the dry side of the island.

The center of the United States is a large open plain. Weather moves across the central plains with nothing to stop it.

Air

Clouds can bounce heat away from the land or hold heat in and keep it from escaping. Cloudy places that already have cold climates will be all the colder from having clouds bounce the sun's heat away. Cloudy places that already have warm climates will be all the warmer from the heat the clouds hold in.

Smoke and heavy gases from burning also trap heat. They let the sun's warmth in but then keep it from escaping. The earth becomes like a closed-up car on a sunny day. The climate can change from these heavy gases.

Water

Water near a place can affect the climate. For one thing, water changes temperature more slowly than land. Land that is near lakes, bays, and oceans will warm up and cool off more slowly than other land.

The effects can be surprising. In Great Lakes cities such as Duluth, Milwaukee, Chicago, Detroit, Toledo, and Cleveland, houses a block from the lake sometimes have sweater weather in winter while a mile away people are putting on their heaviest coats! Then in summer, people in the houses near the lake sometimes need covers to keep warm in bed while families a mile away are having lemonade on their porches at midnight because it's too hot to sleep!

On the seacoasts, water may carry warmth from faraway places and affect the climate. Follow this on a map or globe: Warmth from the South Pacific Ocean flows up past Japan and washes down the Alaskan coast to Washington, Oregon, and California. This warmth keeps the winters in these places much warmer than they might be.

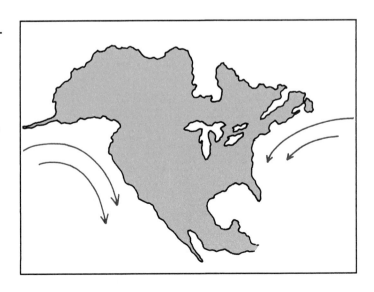

Field Trips

- Research the location of the nearest planetarium or observatory. A planetarium is designed to receive the public on a regular basis; it displays projected images of stars and planets and usually has permanent exhibits. There is almost always an admission charge. An observatory is an academic research institution, usually attached to a university, that may or may not be prepared to receive visitors. There are rather more observatories than planetariums, so if there is no planetarium nearby, one must take one's chances with an observatory. Some observatory directors will be eager to help and others will politely decline even a visit. Some may keep quite irregular hours. An observatory, if you gain admittance, will provide a closer look at an astronomer's equipment since it is an astronomer's workplace, but there are unlikely to be any explanatory displays.

- A seismology laboratory is an academic institution that conducts research on earthquakes and related phenomena. Some are equipped to receive visitors, especially if the laboratory receives public funding. At a seismology laboratory, your student will have a chance to see how the earth is studied and what the equipment looks like. The experience can be unforgettable and eye-opening even for an adult. A telephone call to the geophysics department of a university can help you learn whether there is a seismology laboratory near you that receives visitors.

- One of the simplest astronomy field trips is literally a trip to a field—on a cloudless night away from town lights. The lights of even an isolated town of 10,000 can reduce the number of visible stars by more than one-half, and if you live in a city of more than 100,000, you may have to drive 150 miles to appreciate how the Milky Way got its name. All the same, what one loses in profusion one gains in focus: it is easier to see the main stars that form the constellations when the dimmer stars cannot be seen. Unfortunately, three of the stars that are the first to be obscured by city lights are in the Little Dipper. Take a star chart and a flashlight and identify as many constellations as you can. Prepare for the trip by learning where to look for each constellation at the time of night and time of year of your field trip.

- There are weather stations in various parts of the country, often at airports, but also at other strategic locations. Some monitor weather with direct instruments that measure wind direction and velocity, temperature, humidity, and precipitation. Others are merely satellite receiving stations that receive signals transmitted by weather satellites. You may be able to arrange a visit with one near you.

- If your local radio or television station has a weather reporter, it also probably has a weather department. In the interest of public relations with their viewers, they may permit a visit to the station during which your student may learn where the weather information comes from and how it is displayed.

- A university near you may have a meteorology department or climatology department or astronomy department. More than likely there will be no formal provision for visitors, but it may be fairly easy to get permission to see some student work in progress and get an explanation. You may get permission to look at some of the equipment close up.

Unit 3 Review

With each fill-in, follow this procedure: (1) read each sentence twice with the answer; (2) tell the student to listen for your pause and say the word that belongs; (3) read the sentence again and pause instead of saying the **boldface** word in red. The student is to say the word that completes the sentence correctly.

1. There are **nine** planets in the solar system.

2. The sun is made mostly of **hydrogen.**

3. Most of the earth's surface is **under water.**

4. Day and night happen because **the earth spins around.**

5. A group of stars that look near each other form a **constellation.**

6. A group of stars that are near each other form a **galaxy.**

7. A star is **a globe,** like the sun.

8. The different shapes the moon makes are called the moon's **phases.**

9. A cloud is made of **tiny water drops.**

10. The three main shapes of clouds are **cirrus, stratus,** and **cumulus.**

11. The seasons happen because **the earth goes around the sun.**

12. The sun's light is filtered and weakened by **the air.**

13. Temperature is measured with a **thermometer.**

14. The scientific names of wind speeds, in order, are **breeze, gale,** and **wind storm.**

15. Climate depends on **the strength of the sun's rays, what kind of land is near, what the air is like,** and **what kind of water is near.**

16. Rain clouds can be trapped by **mountains.**

ntetf

Unit 3 Checkout

Answer the questions.

1. Name two things that climate depends on.

2. Name two main shapes of clouds.

3. Why do the seasons happen?

Fill in the blanks.

4. The different shapes the moon makes during a month are called the moon's _____.

5. A cloud is made of _____.

6. A group of stars that **look** near each other is called a _____.

7. There are _____ planets in the solar system.

8. Most of the earth's surface is under _____.

Circle **Yes** or **No**.

9. The sun's light is filtered and weakened by the air. **Yes** **No**
10. Rain clouds can be trapped by a river. **Yes** **No**
11. A group of stars that **are** near each other is called a galaxy. **Yes** **No**
12. Temperature is measured with a **thermometer.** **Yes** **No**
13. The scientific names of wind speeds, in order, are **breeze, gale,** and **wind storm.** **Yes** **No**
14. Day and night happen because the earth goes around the sun. **Yes** **No**
15. A star has five points. **Yes** **No**
16. The sun is made mostly of coal. **Yes** **No**

Assist the student with the reading and writing, but leave the student free to choose answers alone. Decline to supply answers kindly. The answers are on page 124.

Unit 4

The Glory of God's World

Unit 4 explores forms of life on earth, the creatures of the fifth and sixth days of creation. The focus is on animal life: what distinguishes animals from other living things, the kinds of animals, and the different forms of animals bodies. Some microscopic life forms are presented here briefly, and basic concepts of nutrition are introduced.

Chapter 26, on kinds of animals, may be too challenging if presented in too much earnest. In order to convey the large variety of life forms, some concepts of taxonomy are used. It is not expected that a kindergartner will understand taxonomy! Rather, the student should come away from the presentation with the impression that there are a dizzying number of kinds of animals.

By the end of unit 4, the student should have grasped

- The five categories of living creatures
- A few very basic principles of biological classification
- Some differences between the warm-blooded and the cold-blooded animals
- Some basic characteristics that distinguish mammals, birds, insects, and fish from each other and from other animals
- Some concepts about the microscopic organisms
- Some principles of good health and nutrition

You may want to take a moment to review how the learning has progressed to this point. Was the unit review sufficient for the student to recall the material that had been covered in the lessons? If the student missed several questions or it seems that the student merely memorized the answers in the unit review and is still a bit uncertain about the concepts behind the words, consider introducing more frequent reviews. You may quickly go over the material at the end of each lesson before continuing to the next. Sometimes the time lag between lessons presents a problem for the student: if lessons have been presented once a week, consider presenting the lesson in two or three stages on separate days. Some students may benefit from reviews after two or three lessons instead of waiting until the end of chapter 31 of this unit.

Again, watch for special interest on the part of your student. Of course you already know as a parent that interests come and go throughout childhood as a child explores the world and his own talents. Pushing too much may distract a child from his own gifts in an effort to please—but the exploration is to be encouraged, no matter how quickly the student passes from consuming interest to consuming interest.

"And God said, Let the waters bring forth abundantly the moving creature that hath life, and fowl that may fly above the earth in the open firmament of heaven. . . . Let the earth bring forth the living creature after his kind, cattle, and creeping thing, and beast of the earth after his kind. . . . Let us make man in our image, after our likeness: and let them have dominion . . . over all the earth."
—Gen. 1: 20, 24, 26

Focus

God made us with bodies. This means we need to eat and breathe and take care of ourselves. Animals have bodies too, but their bodies are different from ours. Still, animals need to eat and breathe and take care of themselves too.

Connect the dots to find out what animal is here.

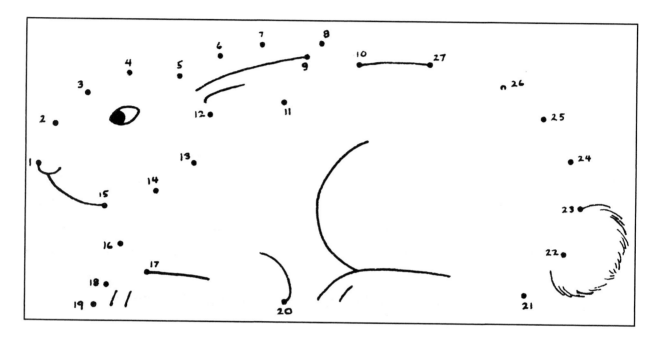

Now draw pictures of your two favorite animals. What do you like about them?

Remember that the purpose of the activity is to focus the student's attention. The drawings may be as humorous, imaginative, or everyday as the student chooses as long as they relate to the topic.

How Scientists Sort

For hundreds of years scientists tried to fit creatures into the three groups of animal, vegetable, and mineral. The more strange creatures they found, the unhappier they became with their groups. Scientists today think it is more helpful to look at how much alike creatures are and put similar things together. Scientists use these five big groups: (1) viruses and bacteria (germs); (2) tiny, almost invisible plants and animals; (3) mushrooms, molds, and yeast; (4) plants; and (5) animals.

The Trouble with Sorting

You need:
- a box of crayons of 64 or more colors

Sort out a large box of crayons into color groups. Start by putting the reds, blues, and yellows together. Leave the other colors out for now.

Now make groups of purples, greens, and oranges. Did you have to think again about any of the other groups? There are no right and wrong answers here. Just keep going.

What will you do with white and black? Will you put them together in one group? Will you make two new groups with only one crayon in each? Any others left? Will gray go with black or white? Do you have silver, copper, and gold? Do you want to make more special groups? How happy are you with your groups?

Now imagine you and a friend had to stay in separate rooms and come up with the same answers to all these questions. Do you think your groups would match perfectly?

You can tell a cow from a rock. Maybe for a moment you might think a stick is a snake or a snake is a stick, but not for long. Once the snake moves the answer is clear. What gets tricky is **naming** the differences between animals and others of God's creatures. Animals are alive, but so are plants. Animals move around, but a plant that traps insects like the Venus's-flytrap moves more than animals like barnacles, which spend their whole lives attached to a rock or the bottom of a ship.

 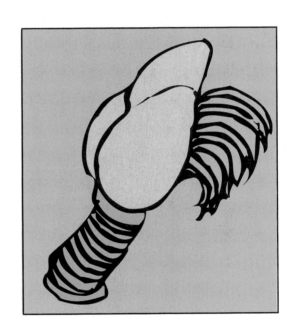

Here is one set of problems scientists have had: Opposums and kangaroos, when they were first discovered by scientists, were hard to put in a group. Their babies are born very small and weak, and then crawl through their mother's fur to a pouch. The babies get milk from their mother's body inside the pouch. They live in the pouch until they are big enough to climb out and hang on their mother's fur.

The problem this made was that opposum and kangaroo babies were very much like mammal babies—say, kittens or puppies. But they were different enough to make scientists wonder. There is another animal something like opposums and kangaroos in Australia called a platypus that lays eggs! Scientists had to make a new group of mammals for these creatures.

Grouping Creatures

Put a check to label each creature as an animal, a plant, or something else.

Creature	Animal	Plant	Other
1. Raccoon			
2. Tree			
3. Spider			
4. Starfish			
5. Mosquito			
6. Water lily			
7. Eel			
8. Mushroom			
9. Butterfly			
10. Cactus			

Chapter 26
Kinds of Animals

One of the jobs God gave Adam was a very big one: to name all the animals. If Adam finished the job (the Bible does not say), his work has been lost, and scientists are still trying to finish naming the animals.

Scientists group animals by their body shapes and parts. Mammals (1) are warm-blooded, (2) have hair, (3) give birth to live babies, and (4) feed their babies milk. Birds (1) are warm-blooded, (2) have feathers, and (3) lay eggs; (4) their babies eat what the adults eat. Insects (1) are cold-blooded, (2) have bony shells instead of skin, and (3) lay eggs; (4) their babies look completely different from the adults. Fish (1) are cold-blooded, (2) have scales, (3) lay eggs, and (4) they breathe water. We will look more closely at these kinds of animals later.

To show just how many kinds of animals there are, let's start with the night crawler or earthworm. There are 1,800 kinds of earthworms. These 1,800 kinds of earthworms are **some** of the 3,200 worms that (1) live on land and (2) have bodies that are divided by rings. There are three other groups of land worms that have ringed bodies.

Land Worms with Ringed Bodies (3,200 kinds)

There are two other groups of worms that have ringed bodies, or three groups in all: (1) ocean worms whose bodies are ringed, (2) leeches, and

(3) land worms whose bodies are ringed. In all, there are 9,000 kinds of worms whose bodies are ringed.

Worms with Ringed Bodies (9,000 kinds)

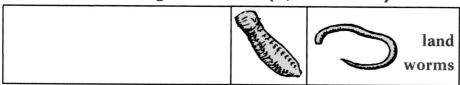

Then there are nine other groups of worms without rings.

Kinds of Wormlike Animals (thousands and thousands of kinds)

								ringed bodies

There are, besides these ten groups, ten other groups of animals that are very wormlike but are not worms at all. Here are nine kinds of animals that are **not** wormlike:

1. sponges
2. octopuses, snails, clams, and their cousins
3. certain shelled sea animals that are very different from both clams and lobsters
4. corals and animals like them that live joined in groups
5. jellyfish and their cousins
6. a group of animals very like jellyfish
7. starfish and their cousins
8. insects, spiders, crabs, and their cousins
9. animals with spines

So all animals fit into about 30 large groups. The ones we know better than any others are in the last nine groups. The animals that we know best are those with spines. Some of them have very soft spines that have no bones. Animals that have backbones like ours are the fish; frogs and their cousins; snakes and other reptiles; birds; and mammals.

On the next two pages are pictures of animals in the last nine groups. Match the groups with the pictures by writing the number of the group (1 to 9). You will use some numbers more than once.

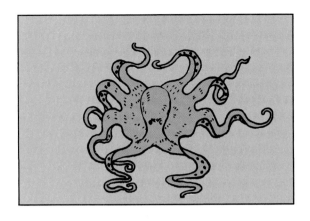

_____

_____

_____

_____

_____

_____

_____

_____

_____

_____

_____

_____

Chapter 27

Mammals and Birds

One of the big differences between some animals and others is the way they stay warm. Some animals make their own heat. Some must find a warm place to get warm. Of course any animal **can** get warm in a warm place. But some animals **must** go to a warm place to get warm.

On a cold night, are your sheets sometimes cold? Does it take a while to warm them up? What warms them up? Think about this.

Are you done thinking? Did you think that your body warmed the sheets? That is the right answer. Now how could your body do that?

If a lizard climbed into your bed with cold sheets, instead of the sheets getting warm, the lizard would get cold! Lizards are one of the animals that must get their warmth from warm places. You make your own warmth.

Cats and dogs and people can run and jump and play in the cold weather, even in the snow. A lizard, a frog, a fish, or an insect could not. In fact, these animals cannot even move unless the air around them is warm enough.

If you ever can catch an insect and put it in a jar, you will be able to see that this is true. If you leave the jar with the insect in the refrigerator for 5 minutes, you will find that the insect is now moving very slowly. Leave the jar out to warm for 5 minutes, and the insect will move quickly again.

(Do not do this more than once with a single insect. The insect could get very sick. And better not to do it even once with a more complicated animal such as a frog or lizard or fish.)

Creatures that do not make their own heat are called **cold-blooded.** Some groups of animals with backbones are cold-blooded. These are sharks and their cousins; fish; frogs and toads and their cousins; and reptiles.

Creatures that make their own heat are called **warm-blooded.** Two groups of animals with backbones are warm-blooded. These are birds and mammals.

Mammals

There are five important differences between mammals and other animals with backbones:

1. hair
2. babies born alive (no hatching)
3. warm-blooded
4. babies fed with milk
5. large brain

Birds

There are four important differences between birds and other animals with backbones:

1. feathers
2. babies hatched from eggs
3. warm-blooded
4. no teeth

Look at the pictures. Write **B** underneath if the picture shows a bird.
Write **M** if the picture shows a mammal.

_____

_____

_____

_____

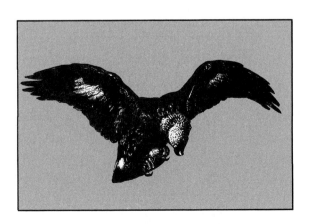
_____

_____

You will probably hear this many times in your school work. You may already have heard it once or twice. Or maybe this is the first time.

Insects are not the only kind of small animals with hard shells. Millipedes, centipedes, and spiders are three other kinds. Millipedes, centipedes, and spiders are not insects.

There are six important differences between insects and similar animals.

1. cold-blooded
2. 3 body parts
3. 3 pairs of legs on middle body part
4. 1 or 2 pairs of wings on middle body part
5. antennae
6. hard shell instead of bones

The Importance of Insects

It is hard to say enough about the importance of these little creatures. Most are not pretty to look at, even though some are very beautiful. Mosquitoes and flies are hated pests, even though God has given them important parts to play in His world.

Insects help clean up other animals' garbage. Insects help plants make seeds and also help plants put the seeds in the ground. And some insects help get rid of pests.

Bees are insects that make food for us. Silkworms are insects that give us cloth. Fine furniture and sailboats are often protected by shellac, which comes from an insect.

The Problems with Insects

We humans also have many problems with some insects. Termites and some kinds of ants ruin the wood in our houses. Farmers often have their work ruined by insects that damage growing plants. Some insects carry diseases.

Insect Life

Most insects begin life as eggs. After they hatch, different insects grow up in one of three ways, which we can call **Complete Change, Partial Change,** and **No Change.**

Insects that grow up with no change simply get bigger. Remember that insects have hard shells, though. So as the insect outgrows a shell, the old shell splits and the insect climbs out of it and grows a new, bigger shell. Silverfish grow like this. Insects in this group have no wings.

Insects that grow up with partial change stay mostly the same through most of their lives. These insects, too, change shells as they get bigger. Then, when they become adults, these insects have a single partial change. Their colors and shapes usually change, and they grow wings. Grasshoppers, beetles, and dragonflies grow like this.

Insects that grow up with a complete change start out wormlike or caterpillarlike and shed many skins as they grow. Then, when they become adults, they change completely in shape and color. Sometimes they form a cocoon or something like a cocoon when they change. Butterflies, beetles, flies, and bees grow like this. Some of the adults of some insects in this group have no wings. (Ants are like this.)

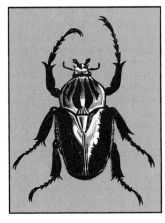
BEETLE

DRAGONFLY

BEE

112

Label the picture **I** if the creature is an insect. Remember the six ways to tell if a creature is an insect.

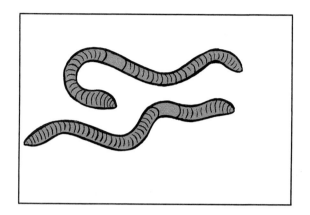

———

———

———

———

———

———

Chapter 29
Fish

We use the word **fish** to talk about many water creatures that are not alike at all. For example, starfish and shellfish are nothing like true fishes. And a silverfish is an insect.

The picture is a little simpler if we say we are talking only about water animals with eyes, tails, and fins. Whales, seals, and porpoises are water animals with eyes, tails, and fins, but they are mammals, not fishes. We can leave them out if we say we are talking about **cold-blooded** water animals with eyes, tails, and fins.

The picture is still a little hard to understand because true fishes can be so different from each other, and creatures that are not fishes can seem more like true fishes. Eels are really fish, but it takes more than one look to see why. There are true fishes that have lungs and can breathe air. Catfish do not have scales like other fishes. Stingrays and other rays are not what we think of as fish-shaped.

If we don't ignore the unusual fishes, though, we can not talk about fishes at all. So we need to agree that when we say **fish** we mean (1) cold-blooded (2) water creatures (3) with backbones that (4) have tails and usually have (5) eyes, (6) fins, and (7) scales of some kind.

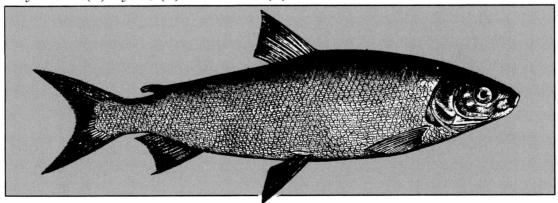

Fish are important as food to many people in the world. They are an important part of the way the world works together, if only because there are so many of them and so many kinds of them.

Fish: Very Much the Same, Very Different

There are as many kinds of fishes as there are kinds of land animals. There may be more things the same between fish bodies than between land animal bodies. But that is because to live in the sea there are strict "rules" to follow if you want to live. The "rules" are not so strict on the land in many ways.

See if you can understand this. It may take some hard thinking. Imagine dropping an elephant into the middle of an ocean. Will it live? Then imagine dropping a mother elephant and a father elephant into the middle of the ocean. Will they live long enough to have babies? If they do have babies, will the babies live? If the babies live, will they live long enough to have babies of their own? Then, can fish live in a desert?

A creature cannot live in a place for which it is not built to survive. What a creature needs to survive in a place makes a kind of "rule" for living there. To live in a desert, an animal must be built to take high heat and be able to go without drinking. To live in mountains, an animal must be able to get over or around rocks, breathe thin air, and take the cold.

Animals that end up in the wrong place die, or else their babies die. Maybe an elephant did wander into the sea once long ago—maybe even a whole herd. But they would eventually have died because elephants are not built to live in the sea. An elephant cannot grow fins, learn to breathe water, and have and do the other things a creature needs for life in the water. So we do not find elephants living in the sea.

The sea's "rules" are many and are fairly strict. In the sea, animals must move by swimming. (There are one or two that have other ways, but we will not study this now.) So fish and other sea animals almost always have fins. Swimming also is easier with a long, slim body, so fish and other sea animals almost always have long, slim bodies.

Animals in the sea must usually get their air directly from the water. So fish and most other sea animals have **gills** instead of lungs, which can take air from the water.

One last thing. Do you know any twins, or any brothers that are so alike or sisters that are so alike that people are always mixing them up? Maybe people you don't know well always mix you up with your brother or sister.

Another one: Do you and a friend have the same toy—the same doll or action figure or truck or book? Probably you do. But can't you and your friend always tell whose is whose? (By that one particular scratch or dent or bump.)

Isn't it easier to see differences between things or people you know well than between things or people you don't see often? To a fish, maybe land animals look all alike because they all seem to have mouths and dry skin and tails and legs. And to a fish, it may be obvious that a shark and a whale have so very many differences it would be hard to see anything at all the same between them.

This is all to say that a close look shows that a herring and a shark are as different as a tiger and a hawk.

With minimal coaching, your student may consider the facts and realize that it is no "accident" that each creature has just what it needs to fit its environment. There is an important opportunity here to lead the student to realize that, since each creature is perfectly suited to live in its environment, we can know that there is a **plan** to life, a design, which strengthens our faith in the Master designer, our God, who has created each creature with skill and beauty.

"Don't put that in your mouth! It has germs!"

Germs is not a word that a scientist would use. The creatures that people call germs are too different to have only one name. And the name itself means "seed," because long ago people thought they were some kind of seeds that maybe grew into some kinds of animals. You may not be surprised by now to hear that there are many thousands of kinds of animals that people call germs. Most often, they are one of two groups, **bacteria** (back-TEA-ree-uh) and **viruses** (VIE-rus-uz).

Bacteria

Bacteria are very tiny creatures that live everywhere on earth, even around and on and in earth's plants and animals—and us. Almost half a million bacteria would fit on a period on this page. Bacteria have one of three shapes: balls, sticks, or spirals. There are bacteria that help us and bacteria that harm us. Most bacteria neither help us or harm us.

Here are examples of good things bacteria do:

1. Because of bacteria, soil has things that plants need to grow. Without plants on the land, land animals would die.

2. Cows cannot really digest grass. One kind of bacteria lives in a cow's stomach and digests the grass for the cow. Then the cow's body can use it.

3. Some medicines come from bacteria.

4. One kind of bacteria makes cheese.

Your skin and the lining of your mouth, throat, and stomach keep bacteria out. When bacteria do find a way in, through a cut or a tear, your body has "guards" that lock up the bacteria or kill them.

Your body usually has a problem only when it is weakened (by being overtired, when you are already sick) or when too many bacteria enter your body at once.

People who have diseases caused by a bacterium may be given an **antibiotic** that kills the bacterium or weakens it so that the body can fight it and get rid of it.

Viruses

There are no viruses that help us, but not all of them harm us. Scientists still are arguing about whether viruses are alive. Viruses can live only by becoming part of a person, an animal, a plant, or a bacterium.

Viruses are a great deal smaller than bacteria. Not being exactly alive, the body does not kill them to get rid of them. No medicines have been found to help get rid of them. The body has to do the work itself.

Before a person becomes sick from a virus, some medicines can teach the body to get ready to fight the virus. These medicines are the shots you get at the doctor's office when you go for a checkup.

Keeping Healthy

There is no way to avoid bacteria and viruses. The goal is not to keep away from all bacteria and viruses. Rather, the goal is to keep from giving our bodies more than they can handle.

These are ways we keep from giving our bodies too many bacteria or viruses:

- Washing our hands several times a day, especially before we eat and after playing with pets
- Using a new cup or breaking off a piece to share drinks or treats with friends
- Making visits to sick people short and avoiding a lot of close contact
- Not using other people's dishes or silverware

- Never eating or drinking anything unless we know where it has been, especially something that is not wrapped
- Never putting anything dirty in our mouths

Here are ways we protect others from getting sick from our bacteria and viruses:

- Covering our mouths when we cough
- Using handkerchiefs or tissues when we blow our noses and sneeze
- Not spitting except in the toilet
- Washing our hands often, especially after using the toilet
- Using a new cup or breaking off a piece to share drinks or treats with friends

Learning about God's World

Bacteria and viruses grow by doubling. One becomes two after a split second, then two become four. Different bacteria and viruses take different amounts of time, but this activity can give you a general idea of what happens and how quickly it happens.

You need:
- a box of rice
- checkerboard

Let's say each square represents a second. Since there are sixty-four squares on a checkerboard and sixty seconds in a minute, the whole checkerboard will stand for about a minute.

To start, one bacterium enters your body. Put one grain of rice on the first square. After one second, there are two. Put two grains on square 2. Double again: Put **four** grains one square 3, then eight, sixteen, thirty-two, and so on. (You may need help figuring the doubles. Your helper may need the help of a calculator after a while, too!)

Keep going as long as you can. You will quickly run out of rice if you have the patience to keep going!

By square 21, you are at 1 million grains—probably more than is in the box. By square 42, you have reached a trillion grains—more than a million boxes of rice, which would be 500 tons! You would need to put the entire world's production for thirty years on square 64.

Your body uses different foods for different reasons. The best way to keep a healthy body is to eat many kinds of food. No one food can be eaten all the time without causing problems. To make sure your body gets all the right ingredients, follow the serving suggestions in the four food groups:

1. Dairy foods—3 to 4 servings every day

2. Meats, beans, fish, or eggs—2 or more serving every day

3. Fruits and vegetables—4 or more servings every day

4. Grains—4 or more servings every day

Dairy Foods

Dairy foods are milk and foods made from milk such as cheese, butter, yogurt, and ice cream. They all build your body, give it energy, and make strong bones and teeth.

Dairy foods combined with fruits and vegetables could give you everything your body needs. The only problem is that dairy foods have too much of some things. Milk and butter have too much fat and can clog the flow of blood in your body if you take too much. Cheese has too much salt. Ice cream has much more sugar and fat than is good for you. You must have some dairy foods, but too much is not good.

Meats, Beans, Fish, and Eggs

Meat is the best food for building and repairing your body, but it is high in fat. Fish is very good for the same reasons, and it is usually low in fat, but it does not build your blood as well as meat. Eggs are as good as meat for building your body, but they have a lot of **cholesterol** (coal-LESS-ter-all), which can clog the blood. Dry beans (that is, not green beans) are almost as good for building your body, but they do even less than fish for building up your blood.

Fruits and Vegetables

Fruits and vegetables have many things that allow your body to use foods. Yellow and orange vegetables like carrots, turnips, pumpkins, and squash are good for some of these things. Leaf vegetables like lettuce, kale, spinach, collards, and mustard greens are good foods for certain others.

Grains

Grains are almost enough to live on by themselves. They are mostly good for food energy, but they also can help build your body and help your body use other foods. They are like beans and fish in missing some things your blood needs. You would still need something from the dairy group, too, for strong bones and teeth. Potatoes are not really a grain but are in this group.

Make a Day's Menu

No one food can have all our body needs to be healthy. We need to eat a **balanced** amount of the best foods from each of the four groups. Plan a day's menu so that the total comes out right in each column.

Meal	Dairy	Meat, Beans, Fish, Eggs	Fruit or Vegetable	Grains
Breakfast				
Lunch				
Snack				
Supper				
Total Servings	4	1	3	3

Field Trips

- Chances are there is a 4-H Club near your home. (Even if you live in a large city!) A visit with your students will allow them to see if there are any animal-care activities there that might interest them. There are likely to be interesting brochures and books around on caring for the creatures in God's world. There may even be a display that your students find interesting. Telephone first so you will know what to expect. At the very least it is worth while to make their acquaintance!
- Similarly there is usually at least one County Agricultural Extension office in every county of every state. The agents in the Extension office often have brochures on hand with valuable information on nutrition and health. Sometimes there are brochures geared to a young audience.
- An aquarium, a natural history museum, a zoo, or a model farm is an obvious choice for a field trip. To make sure the student gets the most out of the trip, **prepare.** Telephone ahead of time to find out what is exhibited and what is explained. Get hold of any supplementary information your student may need in order to gain some understanding from the displays. Tell the student ahead of time what there is to be seen and provide some explanations. During

the trip, make a judicious use of "Look there" and "Did you notice this?" After the trip, discuss with the student what was learned.
- Fish hatcheries operated by the U.S. Fish and Wildlife Service often will take the time to explain what they do if arrangements are made in advance. Other fish hatcheries may also accommodate you. As a last resort, try to make arrangements with the owner of a "fisherman's dude ranch" to learn how they care for hatchlings and what the habits and needs of fish are.
- A hospital or a large clinic may be willing to give you and your student a tour to explain how patients are cared for and the precautions taken against disease. Try to see at least one piece of special equipment (EEG, heart monitor) and receive a simple explanation of what it is for.
- A hospital laboratory can be an instructive field trip destination, but it may be difficult to get permission to enter. If you have friends on the hospital nursing staff or if your family physician is sympathetic, you may have a unique opportunity.
- If a nearby university has an entomologist (student of insects) on its biology staff, the professor may be willing to give your student some time. He or she will have specimens in the lab and will be a most informative guide.

Unit 4 Review

With each fill-in, follow this procedure: (1) read each sentence twice with the answer; (2) tell the student to listen for your pause and say the word that belongs; (3) read the sentence again and pause instead of saying the **boldface** word in red. The student is to say the word that completes the sentence correctly.

1. The five big groups of living creatures are **viruses and bacteria, tiny plants and animals, mushrooms and their cousins, plants,** and **animals.**

2. Animals that make their own heat are called **warm-blooded.**

3. Animals that must get their warmth from warm places are called **cold-blooded.**

4. Two warm-blooded kinds of animals are **birds** and **mammals.**

5. A bird **is warm-blooded, has a backbone, has feathers, lays eggs,** and **has no teeth.**

6. A mammal **is warm-blooded, has hair, bears live babies, feeds its babies with milk,** and **has a large brain.**

7. Two cold-blooded kinds of animals are **insects** and **fish.**

8. The animals whose bodies are most like ours are those **with spines.**

9. We can tell an animal is an insect by its **three body parts, three pairs of legs, one or two pairs of wings,** and **antennae.**

10. Three small animals with hard shells that are not insects are **millipedes, centipedes,** and **spiders.**

11. An animal is a fish if it **is cold-blooded, has a backbone, has a tail,** and **breathes in the water.**

12. There are **helpful** bacteria and **harmful** bacteria.

13. Some ways we can keep healthy are **to wash our hands, to avoid close contact with people who are sick,** and **not to use other people's eating tools.**

14. The four food groups are **dairy, meat, vegetables,** and **grains.**

Unit 4 Checkout

Answer the questions.

1. Name two ways we can tell an animal is a fish.

2. Name one cold-blooded kind of animal.

3. Name two ways we can keep healthy.

4. Name one warm-blooded kind of animal.

5. Name two ways we can tell if an animal is an insect.

Fill in the blanks.

6. Birds have _____ teeth.

7. Living creatures are divided into five big groups, which are: viruses and bacteria, tiny plants and animals, mushrooms and their cousins, _____, and _____.

8. The four food groups are _____, meat, vegetables, and _____.

9. The five ways to tell whether an animal is a mammal are that it is warm blooded, has hair, bears live babies, feeds its babies with _____, and has a large _____.

Circle **Yes** or **No**.

10. All bacteria are harmful.	**Yes**	**No**
11. Only human beings have spines.	**Yes**	**No**
12. A spider is an insect.	**Yes**	**No**
13. Animals that make their own heat are called hot-blooded.	**Yes**	**No**
14. Animals that must get their warmth from warm places are called warm-blooded.	**Yes**	**No**

Assist the student with the reading and writing, but leave the student free to choose answers alone. Decline to supply answers kindly. The answers are on page 124.

Unit Checkout Answers

Unit 1, page 31

1. Plastic is the expected answer, but other reasonable answers are acceptable: cloth, copper, leather, concrete, etc.
2. The student should be able to supply two of these three: fuel, heat, air (oxygen).
3. The student should be able to supply one of these two: carry heat, carry electricity. Answers that have to do with melting, "stretching," and polishing are not expected, but are acceptable.
4. up
5. static electricity
6. a surface
7. makes work easier
8. gas
9. magnet
10. solid
11. lightning
12. yes; 13. yes; 14. no; 15. yes; 16. no

Unit 2, page 63

1. The student should be able to supply one of these two: grow, use food
2. The student should be able to supply two of these four: iron, gold, baby powder, salt. Several other mineral products were mentioned or pictured in chapter 9 (page 35) and are acceptable answers.
3. The student should be able to supply one of these two: plants, proper plowing
4. equal
5. an earthquake
6. erosion
7. make food
8. oxygen
9. rain and snow in the mountains
10. topsoil
11. lava
12. no; 13. yes; 14. no; 15. no; 16. no; 17. yes

Unit 3, page 95

1. The student should be able to supply two of these four: how strong the sun's rays are, what kind of land is near, what the air is like, what kind of water is near.
2. The student should be able to supply two of these three: cirrus, stratus, cumulus.
3. The seasons happen because the earth goes around the sun.
4. phases
5. tiny water drops
6. constellation
7. nine
8. water
9. yes; 10. no; 11. yes; 12. yes; 13. yes; 14. no;
15. no; 16. no

Unit 4, page 123

1. The student should be able to supply two of the following four ways: a fish is cold-blooded, has a backbone, has a tail, and breathes in the water.
2. The student should be able to supply one of the following two: fish and insects. Unexpected but acceptable answers are reptiles, amphibians, and any more specific class of animals of those four classes, such as mosquitoes, perch, turtles, or salamanders.
3. The student should be able to supply two of the following three: washing our hands, avoiding close contact with people who are sick, and not using other people's eating tools.
4. The student should be able to supply one of the following two: birds and mammals. Answers that name a more specific class of animal are also acceptable.
5. The student should be able to supply two of the following four ways: its three body parts, three pairs of legs, one or two pairs of wings, and antennae.
6. no
7. plants; animals
8. dairy; grains
9. milk; brain
10. no; 11. no; 12. no; 13. no; 14. no